MANAGEMENT DEVELOPMENT BEYOND THE FRINGE

MANAGEMENT DEVELOPMENT BEYOND THE FRINGE

A practical guide to alternative approaches

Phil Lowe and Ralph Lewis

Kogan Page Ltd, London
Nichols Publishing Company,
New Jersey

This book is dedicated to David, Joshua, Ruth and Sophie, who have long perfected the art of rejecting assumptions

First published in 1994

Apart from any fair dealing for the purposes of research or private study, or criticism or review, as permitted under the Copyright, Designs and Patents Act, 1988, this publication may only be reproduced, stored or transmitted, in any form or by any means, with the prior permission in writing of the publishers, or in the case of reprographic reproduction in accordance with the terms of licences issued by the Copyright Licensing Agency. Enquiries concerning reproduction outside those terms should be sent to the publishers at the undermentioned address:

Kogan Page Limited
120 Pentonville Road
London N1 9JN

© Phil Lowe and Ralph Lewis, 1994

British Library Cataloguing in Publication Data

A CIP record for this book is available from the British Library.

ISBN 0 7494 1076 0

First published in the USA in 1994
by Nichols Publishing, PO Box 331, East Brunswick, New Jersey 08816

Library of Congress Cataloging-in-Publication Data

Lowe, Phil.
Management development beyond the fringe: a practical guide to alternative approaches / Phil Lowe and Ralph Lewis.
p. cm.
ISBN 0-89397-397-1 : $32.95
1. Communication in management. 2. Work groups. 3. Career development. 4. Interpersonal relations. I. Lewis, Ralph.
II. Title.
HD30.3.L69   1994
658.4 07124--dc20

Typeset by Saxon Graphics Ltd, Derby
Printed in England by Clays Ltd, St Ives plc

CONTENTS

CHAPTER 1

Introduction and Overview

1 INTRODUCTION AND OVERVIEW

It now seems to be an accepted strategic fact that the nineties organization is going to be lean, fit, flat, flexible, adaptable, and full of empowered and innovative employees working together in super-productive cross-functional teams. Does this sound like your organization?

Apart from the occasional model company held up as an example of the way forward, most organizations are still struggling with the weightier issues of cultural change. Up and down the country (and beyond) employees are being told that their company is changing; but unfortunately, many are expected to assimilate the new skills they need by some process of osmosis. While some companies set standards for forward-thinking approaches to management development, for many others training, if training is offered at all, is very often along the lines of a teambuilding workshop (to deal with the cross-functional bit) plus a problem-solving workshop (to deal with the innovative bit) with a day on time management (to help you deal with the 12-hour day you have to work now everybody else has been 'downsized').

If this approach to management development is inadequate, it is certainly not the fault of the protagonists. The Management Development manager has a limited budget, and cannot be blamed for spending it on solid, reliable basic skills workshops. And, of course, they get results. Most people going through a training workshop will gain some measure of benefit. But it seems a little paradoxical that in a decade when flexibility and adaptability are supposed to be the norms, our approach to management development often has trouble becoming flexible and adaptable enough to meet the challenge.

The purpose of this book is to open the box a bit on what is fair game regarding inputs to management development initiatives. Edward de Bono, who we are unable to avoid mentioning once or twice in this book, has a bit of a problem with approaches to management which say 'This is the right way because it's the way we've always done it'. He aims to encourage managers to start their creative or problem-solving processes at a point as far away from their everyday lives as possible. In a way, that is what we are trying to achieve.

The theories, models and philosophies which make up the bulk of this book are not particularly original or new. What they should be is *different*. We have gathered together ideas which we personally have found useful as managers, trainers and also as human beings, and pass them on in the hope that our readers will find them as stimulating as we have in terms of coming up with new approaches to developing people to their full potential. Some of the theories we cover – neuro-linguistic programming, for example, or the interpersonal theories of Will Schutz – are already used in management development work, and in such cases we have attempted to demonstrate more holistic applications: in other words, if something already works for teambuilding, can you take it into wider organizational applications?

What we have tried to avoid, however, is simply amassing a collection of intellectual and philosophical flotsam and leaving you to try and apply it to the workplace. If we'd stopped there it would have been easier to publish a reading list and a season ticket to the British Library. Instead we have structured the book to get to grips with some of the salient organizational and managerial issues which companies are now facing.

HOW THE BOOK IS STRUCTURED

The five broad themes which we cover – career management, leadership, communication and teamwork, coaching and counselling, and living with change – are all tackled using the same approach. In each chapter, we follow the same process. The chapter begins with a brief overview of the topic in question and the reasons for its current importance. Each section of the chapter then examines a different aspect of the topic, drawing on one or more of the background models we have used as inspiration – it might be Chinese philosophy, psychological theory or ancient mythology. Whichever model we have chosen for each section is first explained in its own right, and then considered in terms of its practical application to the topic in question. Many of the theories have overlaps or resonances with topics in other chapters, and we have cross-referenced where appropriate.

Each section within each chapter ends with two 'thought-provokers' for the reader. First you will find a list of questions which you should (a) ask yourself, and then (b) consider asking those people for whom you are responsible. Use the questions as starting points to help you develop your own uses for the models we include. (By the way, we don't give you any answers – sorry!) After the questions we provide some guidelines for trainers and developers which look at 'classroom' issues raised by the kind of approaches we describe. Although they deal mainly with training applications, they are not designed just for trainers (we are attempting to get to the heart of the relationship between those who develop managers and the managers themselves), and those who never enter a training room will be able to adapt the ideas for their own purposes. You will also find a reading list in each chapter: this is intended to add depth to the background theories and models we introduce rather than to the topics themselves: you will not find any books on coaching in the 'Coaching and Counselling' reading list, for example. What you will find are books which will take the interested reader further into the psychological or philosophical background of the book.

The organizational perspective of the book is primarily inside-out: we tend to treat organizations as collections of individuals rather than organic bodies in their own right. We recognize, however, the need to acknowledge the perennial trade-off between individual and organizational needs, and for this reason Chapter 2, Career Management, begins the book proper by relating individual career paths to the needs and growth of the organization, using the theories of Charles Darwin, Carl Jung and Elizabeth Kubler-Ross.

In Chapter 3 we consider the need of the modern organization for leaders rather than managers, and look at how individual leaders – whether of organizations, nations or work groups – can develop and grow. Here we draw on military psychology, transactional analysis, mythological heroes, and Zen. Chapter 4 concentrates on the individual in terms of face-to-face dealings with others, and asks how we can maximize the productivity of our one-to-one and team relationships, with suggestions from the theatre and psychologist Will Schutz, among other sources.

Harnessing the power of individuals is the job of the manager, and coaching – which we tackle in Chapter 5 – is an increasingly valued means of doing it. We concentrate on the crucial relationship between coach and subordinate, and how an understanding of each other's motivations can bring positive results. Into our coaching pot we have thrown Chinese yin-and-yang energy, the Alexander technique and more of Will Schutz's interpersonal theory. The final chapter takes us back to that oft-quoted 'turbulent business environment', and looks at what individuals caught up in complexity and change can do to beat a path through the organizational jungle.

One 'hot topic' which readers may have expected to see on this list is empowerment, that magical process by which individual employees discover meaning and value in their working lives by being handed lashings of autonomy and self-determination, in return for commitment to organizational goals and values. As far as we are concerned, the whole book is dealing with empowerment. This is because, contrary to many management thinkers who take a systemic, outside-in approach in which the individual's role is determined by whatever shape the organization ends up in, we focus on the power of the individual to shape his or her own ends, rough-hew them how his or her employer will. After all, when you stand up in front of a class of managers you are dealing with a roomful of individuals with specific individual needs, and their priority will be to find out 'what's in this for me?'

This means that each chapter is written from the perspective of the individual, and deals primarily with what he or she can do with the knowledge gleaned from the theories and philosophies on offer. If you are reading the book as a trainer or developer, it may appear at first glance like a self-help book. This, we can assure you, is deliberate. Resist the temptation to flick straight to the 'Training Guidelines' at the end of each section: you will find just as many ideas for training and development activities by relating the ideas to yourself as an individual: just as psychotherapists only go into private practice after undergoing several hundred hours of therapy themselves, so the people for whom you are responsible will benefit much more if you have found some personal resonance in the goods on offer. And have you ever met a trainer whom you didn't feel would benefit from being told: 'Phycisian, heal thyself'?

Before we begin our explorations, a couple of caveats. First of all, this book does not claim to be the last word on the subject. We have chosen areas which we have personally found useful as triggers to further thoughts, and leave it to the reader to dig out his or her own old school or college essays on Renaissance thinking or Bauhaus to see if they have anything to offer.

Second, and more importantly, we – like most HR people – do not claim to be experts in every field. Anyone can read a book on management and open their own consultancy practice, but the results may be disastrous. There are techniques in these pages which may require specialist help to apply fully. The applications we suggest are designed for the untrained, but for the sake of anyone whose enthusiasm for a particular technique may be kindled, the 'Further Reading' pages will guide you towards appropriate areas of exploration.

Our main hope is that you enjoy, and are stimulated by, this ramble through several thousand years of deep thought. We also hope that you will take the ideas we offer one or more stages further, adapt them and find new uses for them. But please don't regard what is here as written on tablets of stone: and if you do take these tablets, take them with a pinch of salt – it is by challenging and questioning everything set in front of us that, ultimately, we develop, grow and learn.

DRAMATIS PERSONAE

Below are the individuals whose thinking provided the raw material for much of this book:

F Mathias Alexander Australian nineteenth-century Shake-spearian actor whose regular throat problems led to the discovery of the link between posture and overall well-being, and the subsequent development of what became known as the Alexander technique.

Eric Berne The founding father of transactional analysis, a psychological discipline based on Freudian concepts but translated into popular language (so Freud's concept of the Super

Ego, the Ego and the Id became Berne's Parent, Adult and Child). He wrote extensively on the way that individuals play psychological games with each other in order to get what they unconsciously want. He also developed the idea (not his own, originally) of life scripts – the idea that the patterns of our lives are laid down for us in childhood. His aims were to help people to free themselves from these scripts and games and to realize their true potential as free (non-conditioned) individuals.

Edward de Bono   The man who gave us 'lateral thinking', a term which describes the process of going beyond given frameworks and rules rather than accepting them unquestioningly. Once people think beyond boundaries, says de Bono, creativity and original solutions to problems become more possible. He has written several books using these techniques specifically aimed at managers and business people.

Joseph Campbell   Spent his career gathering myths and stories from around the world and isolating their common threads. From these he suggested that there was a pattern in the myth of the hero which is common to all societies. He wrote many books looking at the importance of myth for everyday life as we live it in our modern society. In the USA he became nationally known after a series of TV interviews and is remembered for his phrase 'Follow your bliss'.

Charles Darwin   Earthworm enthusiast whose interest in the unique diversity of fauna in the Galapagos Islands led to a revolutionary theory of evolution which scandalized the deeply religious Victorians – although Darwin was himself a religious man, and post-Victorians seemed more ready to accept the possibility that the earth was not created within a seven-day period.

Norman Dixon   Served in the military and then became a lecturer in psychology. His studies of military leadership show how failure to think beyond the accepted wisdom or conventions of the day led to military disasters. He has since developed this in relation to industrial accidents – especially air crashes – again pointing out the consequences of blind acceptance of unchallenged information. His are among the few studies of leadership which show convincing evidence of original thought and are highly recommended.

Robert Fritz   A partner of a highly successful US-based consulting firm alongside learning organization guru Peter Senge. Fritz himself has developed a highly original system of consulting – structural consulting – and is able to look at concepts of creativity in ways which directly challenge conventional and accepted views of the topic.

Charles Handy   Professor of Organizational Behaviour at London Business School who has regularly displayed a taste for moving away from the conventional in favour of bringing new and radical ideas to the fore. He is probably best known for his book *Gods of Management* in which he uses Greek myths to explain leadership and organizational patterns.

Carl Jung   Originally a disciple of Sigmund Freud, and one of those who split with Freud on the thorny issue of sexuality. Went on to become a distinguished psychoanalyst in his own right: among the highlights of his highly prolific career were his theory of psychological type (seen regularly in organizations in the guise of the Myers-Briggs Type Indicator) and his work on the idea of the collective unconscious, almost a secular version of religion in his proposition that we all somehow share a common unconscious self, which reveals itself in effects such as 'synchronicity' (the 'isn't it a small world?' effect).

Elizabeth Kubler-Ross   A Swiss doctor who worked in the USA after the Second World War. She began to counsel patients who were terminally ill and whose impending death was rarely mentioned until Kubler-Ross started to talk to them. Initially she received much hostility for doing this but, over the years, care for the terminally ill has incorporated many of her insights and methods, including the identification of distinct stages patients go through in their reactions to their condition.

Edgar Schein   One of the world's leading organizational behaviourist writers. His first major psychology work looked at the brainwashing techniques which the Chinese used on American soldiers in the Korean War. He is a professor at the Sloane

School of Management at Massachusetts Institute of Technology and has contributed in-depth understandings of career dynamics and organizational culture.

Will Schutz   First developed his theories and measurements of individuals in small groups in Harvard in the 1950s. In the 1960s he became one of the leading exponents of the 'encounter' movement at Esalen, an alternative centre in California, and aroused much controversy. Since then he has resumed organizational consulting based upon his original theories of the behaviour of groups.

CHAPTER **2**

Career
Management

2 CAREER MANAGEMENT

INTRODUCTION

In this section, we are looking at career management from two perspectives: the individual's management of his or her own career, and the need for organizations to manage the careers of the individuals within them. The former is a crucial area, because an awareness of what you personally want from your career has fundamental implications for the way in which you as an individual relate to the organization of which you are a part; the latter is equally crucial, because the more that an individual can be encouraged to think of his or her role within an organization as a career that is going somewhere, rather than as an interval between the last job and the next job, the better will be the organization's retention of staff, and the better and more wholehearted will be the contribution of individuals to the goals of the organization.

These two perspectives on career management can be considered in tandem, based on the fundamental premise of this book that *organization development and individual development go hand in hand*. The more flexible the organization, the more possibilities it holds for an individual's career development; and the more flexible the individuals within that organization, the more possibilities exist for them to make a rich and varied contribution to the company as a whole.

These twin poles of organizational thinking – the holistic view of the total organization and its diametrical opposite, the view of the organization from the perspective of the individual within it – create a vast and potentially over-complex arena for thinking about career development. For this reason, in this section of the book we will think about the topic with reference to a selection of models of personal and organization development. In each case, the models are not original, but represent different approaches to thinking about the relationship between an individual and his or her environment. By considering them within a business context, we offer them as 'ways into' the problem of matching individual needs to the business needs of a total organization.

The first section takes Darwin's theory of evolution as a way into the relationship between an organization and its constituent individuals; next we apply Carl Jung's theory of personality development to the concept of a career path; and finally we look at the transition curve, a way of plotting the way in which individuals react to career or job changes.

HOW ORGANIZATIONS DEVELOP

WHY DO GIRAFFES HAVE LONG NECKS?

Not a question that Charles Handy wastes much time on, perhaps, but one that disciples of Charles Darwin can dispose of fairly efficiently. Darwin was responsible for the greatest secular evolutionary theory of our age, that of natural selection. For the uninitiated, it works like this...

Consider an imaginary time a few million years ago when giraffes' necks were substantially shorter than they are now. Through competition for food, they began to exhaust their supply of edible leaves – at least those that were within reach: a vast unexploited store of the same leaves still existed, tantalizingly out of reach.

Let's imagine that, through some genetic accident, a handful of baby giraffes dotted around primeval Africa are born with unnaturally long necks. As these giraffes grow, they discover a rich source of food denied to their stunted colleagues. They survive where some others starve. Some of them mate with each other and pass the genes on to their children. More giraffes are now wandering around with longer necks, feeding abundantly on the higher leaves, growing stronger than the shorter-necked giraffes competing for dwindling resources; mating therefore more successfully, and spreading ever wider their long-necked genetic pool. Somewhere along the line (and indiscernibly, as this is all happening over millions of years) the longer-necked giraffes become the only giraffes there are. As a species, they have adapted to their environment. They have evolved through a process whereby a genetic mutation becomes 'selected' by necessities of survival as essential for the species to continue. Result: giraffes have long necks.

The motto of natural selection is 'adapt and survive'. Those species unlucky enough not to mutate productively find themselves staring down the long tunnel of extinction: an example on our doorstep is the giant panda, which has become more choosy over time about the kind of bamboo it eats in an age where human intervention is making that bamboo impossible to get hold of.

What does all this mean for organizations? Leave that question hanging in the air a moment, while we flit to the Massachusetts Institute of Technology for a few wise words from Edgar Schein.

SCHEIN ON

Edgar Schein has contributed a great richness of ideas to modern management thinking. We are concentrating on one of his concepts, that of organizational 'norms'.

Norms are the reference points which form the basis of an organization's culture – that collective set of values and beliefs which determines the way things are done. Schein identified two types of organization norms: core norms and peripheral norms.

Core norms are those values, beliefs and types of behaviour which are central and fundamental to the organization's existence. In most companies, they are the rules which will result in dismissal or disciplinary action if broken. 'Don't steal from the company' is an obvious example of a fairly universal core norm, but there are many examples where one company's core norms may be completely irrelevant to another. Some organizations will regard a man wearing an earring, or a woman wearing trousers, as a violation of its core norms and as calling into question an individual's suitability for continued employment. In other companies teamworking and sociability form the basis of a core norm, and individuals who prefer to work alone may have a very short future within the company.

Peripheral norms are those values, beliefs and ways of behaving which owe more to habit and the tyranny of the majority than to the 'laws' of the organization. In many companies in which all the men habitually wear ties, coming into work without one will not result in dismissal: it will simply be conspicuous as 'different' from what everyone else does.

Timekeeping is another common peripheral norm. In many companies whose core norm is 'our hours are 9 to 5.30' the peripheral norm is 'Everyone here stays after 5.30, and those who don't aren't really loyal to the company.' Anecdotal evidence suggests that on numerous occasions, little real work gets done in such an organization after 5.30: it is simply a tribal test of loyalty and personal 'fit'. The person who doggedly leaves at 5.30 with a clear desk (and conscience) may be made to feel very uncomfortable by pointed jokes or remarks, but the organization as an entity is unable (and probably wouldn't even consider) taking disciplinary action: no core norms have been violated.

Schein took this theory a stage further and looked at four distinct attitudes to organizational norms: these are shown in Figure 1.

The individual who strictly observes both core and peripheral norms Schein termed the *bureaucrat*. This is the person who never rocks the boat, who keeps his or her 'head down' and gets on with the job as specified. He or she is inconspicuous in conformity.

The individual who breaks both core and peripheral norms is known as the *rebel*. This person is unemployable in most organizations since he or she has no interest in following any kind of desirable code of values or behaviour. Individuals who feel their own norms have been violated by an organization (for example, someone who has just been made redundant but is still required to work out a period of notice) may respond with rebel behaviour (bad timekeeping, rejection of authority, sabotage of computer records), since they will no longer care about satisfying even the most basic requirements of an organization that has let them down.

An interesting combination is the individual who keeps the peripheral norms but breaks the core norms. This is the *subversive*, who appears to be a model of conformity, because he or she is behaving outwardly in a way consistent with fundamental

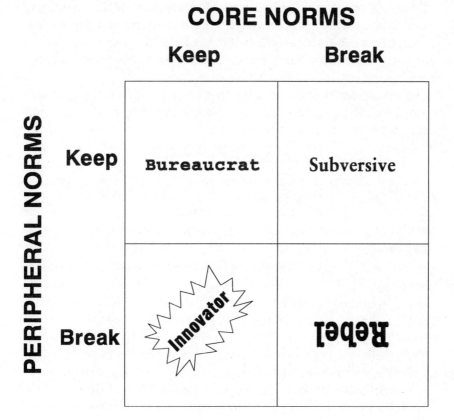

Figure 1 *Attitudes to norms*
Source: © 1993, Harbridge Consulting Group Ltd. Used with
permission.

company requirements; in reality, however, he or she is under-
mining the work of the organization, or working against its best
interests, by disregarding the more fundamental rules and
codes. The 'white collar criminal', the perpetrator of fraud or
insider-dealing, even an employee badmouthing the organization privately to clients – all are examples of subversive behaviour.

The corner of the matrix we are interested in for our purposes is the individual who keeps the core norms but who breaks
some or all of the peripheral norms. Schein termed this individ-

ual the *innovator* and for a good reason: his view was that it is this standpoint which is responsible for organizations changing and advancing, because what the innovator is doing is challenging the habitual assumptions of the organization, while leaving alone the more fundamental assumptions which are necessary for its existence. By questioning peripheral norms, the innovator is able to develop new ways of working which may contribute more efficiently to the core norms of the organization.

TOP DOWN OR BOTTOM UP?

The innovator, to use Schein's term, is also the individual who is responsible for what current research suggests is the way of achieving lasting organizational change: that is, change which happens from the 'bottom up'. (See 'Further Reading' on p44 for more material on this issue.) In Britain we are most used to 'top down' culture change, where a group of senior executives, often the whole board, shut themselves away for a weekend to decide what changes they want, and then return like Moses from the mountain top, waving the New Order above their heads. They then wonder why those lower down the organization appear so resistant to the new ideas.

A textbook example of this is the culture change currently underway at the BBC – the sizeable criticism that was directed at senior executives' decision to closet themselves away in a luxury hotel while they formulated the new vision for the organization was nothing compared to the vitriolic resentment expressed by large numbers of employees when they found themselves on the receiving end of a major organizational change they had had no part in designing. Interestingly, in the second half of 1993 senior BBC managers introduced a policy of organized consultation with groups of employees in an attempt to redress the internal PR balance and to do something about a growing climate of fear in a time of mass redundancy.

One reason for such wholesale resentment on the part of an organization's employees is that the act of drafting a new proposed culture involves lots of people breaking lots of peripheral norms in one go, something which most individuals will find alarming. The governing force of many of our lives is homoeostasis – the force that makes it easier for things to stay the same than for them to change. It is easier to stay in a comfortable bed than to leave it; it is easier to put up with unsatisfactory working conditions than proactively to change them. So it is that an enforced and major 'top down' organizational change will tend to meet with resistance.

The experience of many companies in the USA suggests that what happens in 'bottom up' change is that a small group of individuals in one area of the organization starts working in a slightly different way. They are breaking peripheral norms, but there are only a few of them and the rest of the organization can carry on as normal. However, as this group develops its new working methods, it needs to link to other work units – probably those which form its 'suppliers' and 'customers' within the organization. It needs to persuade and educate these new groups to adjust their working practices to fit this new way. As more and more groups are built into the link, the organization begins to notice the difference. It becomes necessary for senior management to take on board the new practices and attitudes. Eventually the whole organization has adjusted its peripheral norms, but by doing this in bite-sized chunks the process has been relatively painless and hasn't felt much like major change.

OK, so what about natural selection?

GIRAFFE PLC

Let's return to our group of short-necked giraffes pondering the problem of diminishing resources and faced with losing market share in the herbivore sector.

If the giraffes were a typical 'top down' organization, the Board of Giraffe Directors might issue a memo saying: 'The environment out there is changing and we've got to adapt. The leaves are getting higher, our necks are too short, what we need to do is climb the trees so that we can all eat.' The result is open giraffe rebellion: some of the giraffes are frightened of heights; others don't mind the idea, but have never been taught the skills necessary for climbing trees. In any case, their hooves are not particularly suitable. Result: they starve *and* the organization breaks down.

Natural selection brings more of a 'bottom up' approach. Some giraffes, through natural genetic inclination, find themselves able to challenge the norm 'All giraffes have short necks' (we can treat this as a *peripheral* norm, since it is not at the moment a prerequisite for survival). These longer-necked giraffes have found a more efficient way of meeting the organization's *core* norm 'All giraffes eat leaves'; they form genetic networks with other similarly inclined giraffes. The organization begins to change the way it gets its resources.

Eventually, those giraffes who have not adopted the new long-necked approach fall by the wayside; they leave the organization, in this case through death. Result: the organization survives, with a new, culturally entrenched way of working, a new set of peripheral norms ('All giraffes have long necks') and a different workforce population whose attributes match the new working methods.

CULTIVATE MUTANTS

If you follow this line of thought, it is possible to see Schein's innovator as the 'genetic mutant' within an organization: the individual who has a different way of doing things, a different world-view, a different set of peripheral norms. Through a process of natural selection, if you leave this individual to get on with it, one of two things will happen: either his/her unique approach will prove to be more efficient or more valuable than the established set of values, beliefs and behaviour, or it will prove to be unproductive and misguided. Similarly, two sets of reactions from those around the individual are possible: tolerance, encouragement and empathy; or disapproval and rejection. These are represented on the matrix in Figure 2.

The ideal quadrant here is the top left-hand box, representing an organization whose culture encourages the development of new ideas and new ways of working. It adapts to the needs of its business environment through the empowerment of its workforce to challenge assumptions and solve problems in their own way, while being supported by the organization.

The top right-hand quadrant represents an overuse of this policy. If an empowered climate is not policed correctly, an individual may be allowed to pursue unproductive or even damaging approaches to work: like a cuckoo in the nest, the unsuitable

INDIVIDUAL APPROACH

	Productive	Unproductive
Encourage	Adapting for survival	Cuckoo in the nest
Discourage	Doomed to extinction	Systemic alignment

*(Left axis: **ORGANIZATIONAL CULTURE**)*

Figure 2 *Attitudes to organizational mutants*

working practices grow and develop, obscuring the goals of the organization.

At the bottom right of the matrix, the organization is adopting a process of systemic alignment: individual freedom to innovate is set within the context of shared and understood organizational goals, which facilitates the process of weeding out unproductive ideas and approaches.

Overuse of this approach is represented by the bottom left corner. This is the organization which weeds out everything that does not conform to both core and peripheral norms. New

ideas are stifled; individuality is frowned upon. Talk of respon-
siveness and flexibility is usually little more than lip service.
Like a dinosaur, this mighty beast is in danger of finding itself
overtaken by rapid environmental changes.

IMPLICATIONS FOR CAREER MANAGEMENT

For an organization to strike a productive balance between the
top left and bottom right of our diagram, it needs to pay attention to the career values and aspirations of its employees. Again,
a balance is needed between offering individuals the flexibility
to explore their interests and inclinations, and curbing their
worst excesses.

Those managers interested in the retention of staff should
remember that the weeding out process involved in the concept
of systemic alignment does not necessarily represent a straight
choice between retention and dismissal. Often lateral, cross-
functional moves within an organization can enable an individual pursuing a potentially unproductive line in one area of the
company to find his or her niche in another area. Don't forget
that the larger the organization, the more likely it is that different areas and functions will have their own peripheral norms.
(We worked with one finance institution whose norms included
the expectation that people working in the systems function
would dress in a way that broke the dress codes of the rest of
the organization. Thus someone in systems who dressed in a
conventional suit and tie was in the unlikely position of being
seen as an innovator!)

For individuals, it is worth remembering that no one can sack
you for breaking a peripheral norm. If you can develop the
essentially assertive standpoint that everything which happens
is ultimately for the best, then it is possible to allow natural
selection to work for you. This means following your own inclinations and 'being yourself' in your approach to the work you
do, and allowing the organization to decide whether or not you
fit its approach to the outside environment. Even in an extreme
case, if you are squeezed out for being an individual by an organization which cannot tolerate individuality, the gain is ultimately yours; similarly expressing your individuality in an organization for which you are the wrong kind of individual avoids

delaying the discovery that you are following a potentially unrewarding career path.

QUESTIONS

- How diverse is your organization's 'genetic pool'? (Is it prescriptive in its recruitment and development policies, creating an identikit workforce which lacks the potential to adapt? Or does it encourage individual expression in a way which allows it to exploit the unique strengths and contributions of the workforce? Put another way, does it allow giraffes to reach the leaves in their own way, or does it make them all climb trees?)

- Does the organization believe in 'diversity at all costs'? (Is it encouraging a culture which lacks focus by concentrating on doing things differently for the sake of being different? Or are individuals encouraged to tailor their unique strengths to the goals of the organization?)

- Is your personal development being hindered by an obligation to 'follow the rules' rather than explore new ways of doing your job?

GUIDELINES FOR TRAINERS

The most certain way of killing off opportunities for individuals to really develop to their full potential is to provide a diet of training which is little more than a set menu: an organization which is overprescriptive in the skills requirements it sets out for its employees may threaten its own adaptability. On the other hand, the 'carvery' approach to training, where individuals can choose from what is on offer, may lead to a 'cuckoo in the nest' scenario whereby employees are following their own inclinations without considering the ultimate goals and business objectives of the organization.

If you accept the premise that to cultivate employees whose ability to challenge assumptions and refusal to be hidebound by unnecessary guidelines is ultimately to the benefit of the organization, then structured training and development activities need to be built around the dual goals of allowing each individual to understand and develop his or her unique potential while ensuring that the organization's vision and/or business mission are understood and accepted by everyone. This is not a task to be underestimated!

If the culture of your organization already resides in the top left or bottom right of our quadrant in Figure 2, then you (or the organization) are to be congratulated. However, the continual task for the trainer or management developer is the monitoring of the balance that we have discussed. Keeping clear boundaries between various training activities and understanding their role in the development of both the individual and the organization is crucial. This means that the trainer has to be fully aware of the goals and mission of the organization, otherwise it may be difficult to understand and control training activities effectively. He or she has also to be equally aware of the core and peripheral norms in an organization and how training either challenges or reinforces both of these sets of rules.

It is an area where you, as a trainer or developer, may have to make careful political judgements about your own behaviour. In many organizations trainers and developers used to be seen as being on the fringe of the organization and marginal to its mission. One reason for this was the regularity with which training staff would tend to break peripheral norms themselves, and were consequently seen as 'different' and less deserving of power and authority. So the issue of organizational 'mutants' may in many cases be highly germane to the activities and power of the training department: trainers like to think of themselves as 'different', but if they become ostracized rather than (as they may prefer to think) leading the organization forward, a more 'change from within' style of approach may be needed.

One practical starting point for trainers is to place all their programmes or management development activities on a scale with individual focus at one end and organizational focus at the other. Activities can be placed according to their prime objectives and benefits. The ideal is probably a broad spread with a cluster in the middle, representing activities that benefit the individual within the framework of the organization's needs. However, there will always need to be activities focused on organizational needs, and a few activities which exist solely to help individuals on a personal basis, such as employee assistance schemes (although there is a strong case to be made that any such scheme ultimately benefits the organization as well, through an increase in employee morale).

As a trainer, then, ensure you are fully clear about the organization's business and mission, its core and peripheral norms. Then examine where you and the training you conduct are in the light of this – whether training breaks, or encourages others to break, any peripheral norms, and whether this helps or hinders the achievement of individual or organizational goals.

CAREER AND SELF-FULFILMENT

In our last book, *Individual Excellence*, we looked at the impact of psychoanalyst Carl Jung's theory of psychological type on our everyday working lives. This time round, we are more interested in his broader model of personal development, and how it relates to an individual's career path and role within an organization.

Carl Jung was originally a disciple of Freud, but split with him on the thorny issue of what it is we are trying to do in our adult lives. Sigmund Freud held that our behaviour as adults is all about *sublimation* – working out the various issues and complexes left over from our childhood. In particular he held that our 'infantile sexuality' is responsible for many adult complexes and motivations.

Jung was not so sure about the sexual awareness of children, and preferred to see life as working towards a future goal, rather than escaping from nasties in the past. Rather than sublimation, he saw our adult behaviour as driven by *individuation* – the process of making ourselves into individuals distinct from each other.

Jung saw life as a journey during which we search for our sense of *self*. The implication of his theory is that you may never really discover your true self. What you have to make do with in the meantime is the *ego* – your temporary sense of identity (temporary in the sense that it is incomplete for as long as your true self remains hidden).

The ego is, in a way, one half of your true self. It represents your conscious mind. Its complementary half is the *shadow* – the 'dark side' of your personality. 'Dark' in this case does not necessarily mean evil: the shadow is simply all the parts of your personality that remain beyond conscious control; all the undeveloped, primitive bits of you which may pop up when least expected. According to Jung, you discover your true self at the point at which you marry together your ego and shadow – at which you bring all your personality into conscious awareness. This, as you can probably guess, is a tall order for many people, and is one reason why individuation is a tricky process to get right.

To help us deal with the world while we deal with the conflict between the ego and the shadow, we rely, according to Jung, on our *persona*. This, the Greek word for 'mask', is the face we put on for the world around us. It may or may not match what we are like underneath, but compensates for the gaps in our personality while we wait for our ego and shadow to come to an amicable arrangement.

At the heart of Jung's model is the quest for the marriage of two complementary halves: the joining of the ego and the shadow to create the self, for example. Jung also wrote about each individual's quest for a 'spiritual' opposite. Put simply, his theory was that every man carries within him his *anima*, or female image, and every woman carries within herself her *animus*, or male image. Jung's explanation for the attraction of opposites is that we are seeking in the other person our animus or anima.

One of Jung's other preoccupations was with our attitude to impending death. In one of his more cheerful moments, he writes eloquently of the 'secret midday of life', that point at which, unbeknown to us, we are halfway between birth and death. In Jung's view, the mid-life crisis is about coming to terms with, and welcoming, the approach of death, and he felt that those people who overcame this dilemma were the individuals who had successfully made themselves whole.

In more basic Jungian terms, what many psychologists believe happens during the mid-life crisis is that our shadow, or unconscious self, begins to come more into view, and invade our consciousness: but if you're not ready for it, this process can be even more disruptive than having a wholly unconscious shadow side.

MY CAREER, MY SELF

Jung's basic model of personality development mirrors the career path of many individuals. It's possible to view the journey through your working life as a search for your true self. We represent this diagrammatically in Figure 3.

On this model, your onward struggle through different jobs represents a quest for that one job which is 'really you'. In the meantime, your career choices tend to be determined by your ego – which tells you what you *think* you are looking for – but all the time you sense that some other part of you, lurking within, is not really being fulfilled.

This unseen part, your shadow (because it remains unutilized in any productive sense), is apt to take over at vulnerable moments – notably at times of stress. So it is that those working for you may see a different person at work when the pressure is on, or when you have had a lot of unpleasant tasks to deal with.

In the meantime, what people tend to see at work – at least in favourable circumstances – is your persona. This 'work face' is a product of the psychological contract, that unwritten document which represents a compromise between what you want out of work and what your work demands of you. The persona is born also out of company politics, the need to say one thing and think another, and also out of whatever conditioning you may have been subject to in terms of what work is and how we are expected to approach it.

The net result of all this is that your personality, in terms of your relationship to work and career, becomes fragmented. You think one thing, do another, sometimes behave in unexpected and uncontrollable ways, and all the time feel that 'there must be something more'. There is indeed – and you'll find it under your navel!

QUESTIONS

- To what extent do people's jobs within your organization require them to develop undeveloped aspects of their personality? Does the annual appraisal and goal- setting process of the company take into account personal development points? (In other words, do people have an opportunity to develop their shadow side?)

- To what extent does the organization have a code of behaviour which all employees are expected to follow? Do people have to toe the company line, or are they free to explore their own views and approaches within the company? (In other words, are people forced to develop an inflexible persona and lose sight of their ego?)

- Where are you going? (Always better to confront the broad unanswerable questions!)

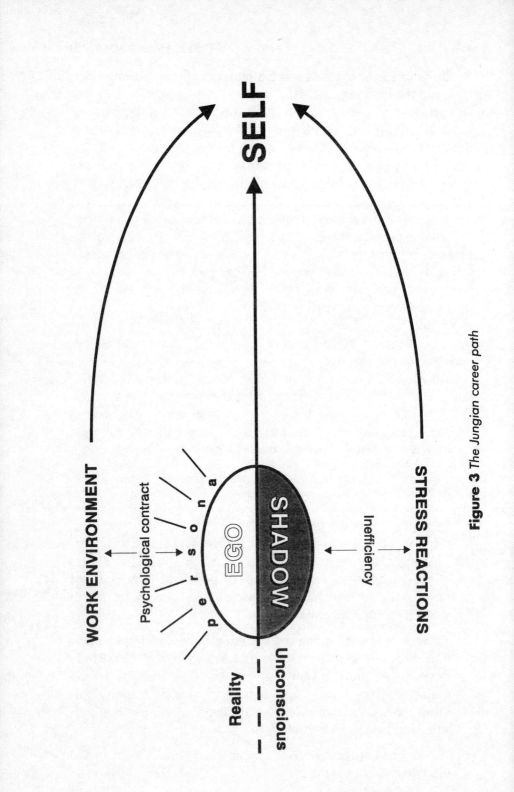

Figure 3 *The Jungian career path*

- How do you react to stress? Do you feel that everything goes out of control when you are 'in the grip' of your shadow? Can you identify the areas which cause you stress? (If you can tackle them directly, you may be able to develop aspects of your shadow side along the way, and help the process of bringing it into conscious awareness.)

- Do you feel valued as an individual within the company? Do people ever see the 'real you'? Or do you perpetuate a work persona which gets in the way of you and what you want for yourself?

TRAINING AND DEVELOPMENT GUIDELINES

Using Jung's model, as we have done, to help illuminate an individual's relationship with his or her career and its development may be more suitable for a one-to-one career development discussion than any formal training activity – although it could be used as the basis of an individual 'workbook' approach to help managers think through the journey on which they find themselves.

The most appropriate starting point for trainers who are interested in using Jungian ideas is to develop a general awareness of the theory involved – the foibles of individuals in a classroom, and the surprises they spring on you as a trainer can then be more readily allowed for. For example, Jung's concept of the shadow – our unknown and unconscious aspects of personality – is of great benefit when someone erupts with anger during a training session. The session itself, or perhaps comments made by you or another participant, will have touched this person's shadow and produced an unconscious and uncontrollable reaction, usually of either fear or anger. It can then be understood not as an intentional personal attack but as something beyond individual control. (Also monitor your own reactions to their outburst: where are they coming from?)

This also applies to decisions made by individuals in terms of their career moves – these are not necessarily the logical conscious consequence of careful planning but are often, according to Jung, the unconscious stirrings of the soul or self as it seeks fulfilment. Anyone involved in training or management development can find opportunities to help individuals grow and develop by understanding and supporting them as they try to come to terms with hidden parts of themselves. The most practical thing you can do is often simply to encourage these individuals to listen to themselves and what their own unconscious is trying to tell them.

CAREER TRANSITIONS

Elizabeth Kubler-Ross made extensive studies of the reactions of terminally ill patients on learning the facts about their condition. When she put her observations together, she found that each and every terminally ill individual went through a series of identifiable stages in the process of coping, or attempting to cope, with the reality of death. Not everybody went through all the stages she identified – the ones who did were those who succeeded in coming to terms with their condition. The seven steps can be plotted graphically as a curve, as in Figure 4.

The vertical axis represents the patient's competence in dealing with his or her condition – put another way, how positive the attitude of the patient is at each stage. Stage one, *Immobilization*, is the immediate reaction to the news: the mental or emotional shock may be fleeting, or may last for several days. The second stage represents a more positive attitude, but the positive feelings are essentially self-deluding, for this is the stage of *Denial*. The stance here is 'It isn't true: the tests must be wrong; there's obviously nothing wrong with me'. Some patients may never progress beyond this stage: death overtakes them before they can be convinced of the truth of the prognosis.

If the patient can be convinced of the reality of the situation, this positive stance is wiped out at a stroke and the patient advances quickly to the third stage, *Incompetence*. At this stage the patient realizes the truth about his or her condition. The overriding feeling is one of impotence: 'I can't cope with this, I might as well give up now.' This is the point at which counselling is usually needed most: if the patient can be persuaded to try to cope he or she can be coaxed into the *Acceptance* stage. Everything is in place for an increase in positive attitude: the patient is prepared to face the reality of the situation.

Being prepared to face reality is one thing; knowing how to face it is a different matter entirely. This makes the next stage essential as the patient enters a period of *Testing* or experimentation. This involves trying different approaches to dealing with the situation, until the one that suits the patient best is discovered. This leads to stage six, a *Search for meaning*, as a result of which the patient develops an understanding which can be built

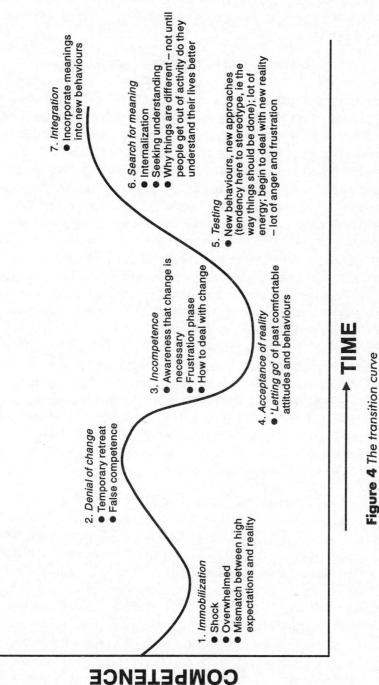

Figure 4 *The transition curve*
Source: © 1993, Harbridge Consulting Group Ltd. Used with permission.

on to complete the curve with the final stage of *Integration* – the lessons learned, and the most successful and suitable approaches, are applied to the patient's situation to produce an effective coping style.

A TRANSITION FOR EVERY OCCASION

Other commentators have been quick to spot the universal applicability of Kubler-Ross's discovery. It has been suggested that every change or life transition we go through causes individuals to pass through the seven stages of the curve. Any readers who are parents will know this only too well. The shock of having a new baby is quickly followed by the denial stage: this baby won't change us, we'll carry on going to dinner parties and take it with us – it's not going to get in our way. It does, of course, and this leads to the incompetence stage: we can't cope, we're obviously not cut out to be parents. The eventual acceptance of the realities of parenthood leads the parents to try out approaches to parenting which suit them best. This leads to an understanding of which kind of role suits each parent; this enables them to achieve an integrated approach to parenthood.

Other positive life transitions which involve this curve include marriage – where the initial denial that anything has changed leads to potential friction but ultimately, hopefully, to true integration. (Divorce, of course, involves exactly the same process, with at least one partner often insisting that things haven't really changed. A rude awakening follows, followed again by a discovery of new lifestyles to cope with the change.)

ANOTHER JOB, ANOTHER CURVE

Studies conducted by one of the authors in the early 1980s looked at ways of applying the received wisdom of the transition curve to career management. It became apparent through different studies that managers starting new jobs, or even being transferred within the same organization, all go through the same seven stages.

The effects of the transition curve can often be seen most clearly in the context of that career intervention which most of us crave but which can be the bane of our lives: promotion. The

Peter Principle, one of the many incontrovertible laws of management, tells us that the reward for competence in a job is promotion to a position that requires even more competence. The process continues until the individual arrives in a position which he or she is unable to fulfil, at which point promotion stops, the individual having risen to his or her own 'level of incompetence'.

As an example, let us look at an exemplary sales rep. His sales figures break all records, his relationship with customers is enviable. So what does the organization do? It promotes him to sales manager. Unfortunately no one has explained to our ex-rep what exactly it is that sales managers do. So once he has got over the shock of promotion, he moves to stage two of the curve and simply denies that any change has taken place. He carries on going out and visiting clients, only this time getting under the feet of the team he is supposed to be leading. If he is unlucky, no one enlightens him as to the potential damage he is doing to the team and himself.

If he is lucky, someone above – or even below – him will point out that he is doing a bad job as a manager. He slides rapidly down the curve to stage three, incompetence. He knows now what it is he is supposed to do – but he also is painfully aware that he can't do what is required of him. It is a tragic and humbling stage: the star salesman reduced to an example of how not to be a manager.

The only thing to be done is to keep going through the curve. Stage four brings an acceptance of the situation and a new realism: 'OK, I'm a manager, I'd better start behaving like one.' The experimentation stage brings an opportunity to find the management style which suits him best: it may involve training in key management skills, or an opportunity to be coached by bosses or peers. An understanding of the appropriate management style and what it means for him personally is followed closely by the final stage: integrating what has been learned into his daily management life.

It sounds easy enough: but there are many factors working against us when we try and go through the entire transition curve. For a start, most of us don't know we're on it. In the management fast-track of many contemporary organizations, high-flying managers being groomed for stardom may move jobs once a year, or more. Since the studies in the early 1980s suggest that it can take eighteen months to two years to go through all seven stages, we can see that many managers are in danger of spending large parts of their careers without ever getting beyond the denial stage: they approach each job as if it is the one they have just left; whether it resembles their previous job or not, that is what they try to make it. Then, just before their incompetence is revealed, they are transferred again – leaving the new incumbent to cope with the detritus his or her predecessor has left behind.

Organizations, too, go through this curve following a change, however small. Consider the purchase of a new computer system. As the operators cope with the shock of an unfamiliar way of working, their instinctive reaction is to use it in the same way they used the old one – they deny that anything has changed. The potential disasters this can cause will only be staved off by convincing the operators to accept their incompetence and to learn and understand the requirements of the new system.

IMPLICATIONS FOR CAREER MANAGEMENT

It is important to recognize the power of the transition curve, and its universal presence. Anyone whose career involves regular moves and changes of role or environment needs to be able to identify the point on the curve at which he or she currently sits. Similarly, organizations who are genuinely interested in the welfare and development of their people must accept that a policy of regular transfers or secondments, despite their potential for sending managers round the learning curve, also send them round the transition curve – possibly without the opportunity ever to reach the end.

It is not just developmental fast-tracks which can cause problems to managers coping with transitions. Many organizations put time limits on success or failure in a particular role: 'You've got six months to sort this place out'. The manager in question may, of course, need six months just to sort him- or herself out, let alone begin to cope with the requirements of a new role. We worked with one retail organization which deliberately operated such a policy: new branch managers would be given a store for a year, at the end of which time the bottom line would determine whether they were kept on or not. Bearing in mind our newfound knowledge about the length of time it takes to go round the curve, we plugged away at the organization until they agreed, as an experiment, to allow two years' trial instead of one. The net result was a much lower turnover of staff, and a cessation of the established boom-and-bust pattern of individual stores' profit figures.

QUESTIONS

- How many changes do you put each of your own staff through in any one year? (And is the justification usually that it will develop and 'improve' them?)

- What kind of support network exists for them as they cope with career transitions?

- Do you 'police the system' to ensure individuals don't stay too long at any one stage?

- Are people clear what is required of them when they are promoted or moved to new positions?

- How long is it since your last career move – whether within your organization or from a different one?

- How do you treat your current role – as an extension of your last one or as something completely different?

- Do you feel competent in your current position?

- Do you understand what is required of you in your current position?

- How many different ways of approaching your current job are you aware of? Do you experiment with them?

- Do you feel 'at home' in your current role? Or do you find yourself thinking how much easier everything was in your last job?

TRAINING AND DEVELOPMENT GUIDELINES

The primary need when dealing with career transitions is for some kind of organization-specific diagnostic to be able to establish with reasonable accuracy the point on the curve at which a given individual currently resides. This might take the form of a questionnaire, or be incorporated into an appraisal or career development interview.

Once an individual's position on the curve has been established, he or she will have a specific kind of training and development need, as suggested below:

1. *Immobilization*   Not too much can be done in this early stage, other than reinforcing the current reality. How this is done depends on whether the shock is a reaction to personal change (such as a new job) or organizational change (such as a change in structure or working practices). In the former case, the reinforcement is probably best effected on a one-to-one basis; in the latter, briefing sessions or focus groups looking at the exact requirements of the current reality may be more appropriate. Even more appropriate though, in both cases, is to anticipate the change and never to assume that individuals will automatically cope positively with something which the organization views as positive. Even a promotion needs extensive preparation if it is to be a genuinely positive experience for all concerned.

2. *Denial*   In many cases, just getting somebody to recognize that they are at this stage will be all that is necessary to move him or her forward. If things are not quite so straightforward (about 999 cases in every 1,000) then the primary job of anyone responsible for the development of the individual in question is to make sure he or she is not storing up too much trouble for him- or herself. This may mean working with the team he or she is now managing to encourage them to be flexible and tolerant in the early stages – and perhaps encouraging them to come and talk to you if they experience any problems as a result of the individual not fulfilling the new role adequately.

    A good high risk/high return strategy is to try and encourage some form of upward feedback session – where the new manager finds out directly or semi-directly the reactions of his or her team to his or her management style. The team may well demand a new set of skills and be able to convince the manager of his or her 'incompetence' (if face-to-face, this needs careful facilitating; if you are the team's messenger, your sensitivity and counselling skills will pay dividends).

3. *Incompetence*   Someone at this stage of the curve needs a lot of support – and they are very unlikely to get it! First, because having promoted someone, say, because of his or her displayed competence, those responsible for the promotion may worry that they are admitting they made a mistake by acknowledging the difficulties caused – or they may feel that it is up to the individual to face up to the challenge of the new position unaided. Second, because in these turbulent times, the number of people undergoing change of one sort or another might

development resources too far if they were all to receive individual attention.

Practical help that training can give – if individual counselling is not an option – is to provide a forum in which those undergoing career changes can get together to provide mutual support. Some kind of structured training activity which reinforces the individual's own abilities, while providing practical help in dealing with stressful situations, would be valuable. If the 'incompetence' is just that – a lack of competence – then a competency-based approach could be taken, in which individual training needs can be assessed and dealt with in groups of people who share a similar need.

4. *Acceptance*   This is a good opportunity for individual, line manager and management development staff to agree a development plan: to do this earlier would be to do it without the consent of the individual, since he or she would not have seen the ultimate value. To do it at this point is to capitalize on the individual's 'potential energy' for dealing with change. A plan needs to be established whose goal is stage seven (Integration) and which on the way contains activities designed to shed any inappropriate behaviours or practices from the previous stages, while embedding those practices which are needed for the individual's new role.

5. *Testing*   Skills-based training in a not-too-structured environment will give the individual the opportunity to try out new approaches while amassing those skills and competencies necessary to deal adequately with his or her role. On-the-job coaching (see Chapter 5) may well be appropriate for many individuals.

6. *Search for meaning/understanding*   If it hasn't already taken place, some kind of off-site development activity involving personality assessment or psychometric testing of one kind or another would be invaluable here. It gives the individual time away from the job to take stock; if a good reliable and non-threatening instrument is used, it gives him or her a framework within which to understand how and why his/her appropriate and inappropriate reactions to the demands of the new role may have occurred. And it will hopefully cement the learning which has taken place by allowing individuals to relate the lessons learned directly to their own personalities.

7. *Integration*   This is the point at which the development plan can be signed off – but its key pointers and learnings should be incorporated into the individual's performance goals for the forthcoming period, to ensure that the lessons are firmly embedded.

FURTHER READING

If you prefer animals to managers, and don't happen to know any Darwinists, Miller, J (1989) *Darwin for Beginners*, McKay, covers the background and basics of natural selection – or you could try Darwin, C (1979) *The Illustrated Origin of Species*, Hill & Wang. For a more organization-based read, Edgar Schein's own book, Schein, E (1978) *Career Dynamics: Matching Individual and Organizational Needs*, will give more insight into his theories of career development.

Beer, M, Eisenstat, R A and Spector, B (1990) 'Why Change Programs Don't Produce Change', *The Harvard Business Review*, Nov/Dec issue, summarizes the bottom-up theory of organization development to which we refer.

In the same series as the Darwin book is the excellent *Jung for Beginners* (Hyde, M and McGuinness, M, 1992, Icon) which puts adequate flesh on the personal development model covered in this chapter. For true enthusiasts, there's always Jung, C (1926) *Psychological Types* (Collected Works, volume 6, Routledge & Kegan Paul). An American book Zweig, C and Abrams, J. (eds) (1991) *Meeting the Shadow*, Jeremy P Tarcher (Los Angeles), is a collection of essays which examines the Jungian concept of the shadow in numerous situations. The most pertinent essay in it is B Shackleton's 'Meeting the Shadow at Work'. And we can't leave the Jungian arena without plugging our own book *Individual Excellence* (Kogan Page, 1992) which takes Jung's personality theory and applies it to the everyday workplace.

The transition curve, as mentioned above, is widely used and applied, but it's almost impossible to obtain any formal material on it. For a different perspective on how we spend our whole lives coming to terms with life, you could try Levinson, D J *et al* (1986) *The Seasons of a Man's Life*, Ballantine, or its less academic (or more readable, as you wish) derivative, Sheehy, G (1984) *Passages*, Bantam.

CHAPTER **3**

Leadership

3 LEADERSHIP

INTRODUCTION

Leadership – or the lack of it – has become a pertinent issue in all areas of society. There has been much discussion on the nature of leadership itself. In business terms, leaders are seen as those individuals who develop a vision and sense of direction for the people or organization they are leading. This process involves the communication of their vision, the inspiring of people and the gaining of their commitment. In other words, true leadership engages the heart as well as the mind: it gives a sense of meaning to what in themselves can be mundane activities.

Leadership often involves actions which are essentially symbolic: actions which bind groups together, but which may have little economic or rational effect. A leader, for example, who takes a pay cut while whole layers of management are being excised from the organization may have made little genuine contribution to cost saving on the scale required by the organization, but is demonstrating a symbolic unity with organization staff. The military analogy is 'I wouldn't ask my men to do anything I wouldn't do myself.' (Military parallels are often used – as we shall see later in the chapter – because, as has been pointed out by other commentators, no one ever *managed* an army into battle.)

Leadership is often defined in terms of the contrast between leadership and management. The latter is predominantly a rational activity which in its purest sense treats an organization as a vast efficient machine. The positive output of this approach is productivity and economies; the negative output is often alienation and a lack of emotional engagement on the part of employees – the 'spirit' goes out of the organization. Over-managed organizations will set the objective of maximizing profits as an overriding priority – and profitability, unless you are a shareholder, is not very motivating to employees.

In any organization there has to be a balance between leadership and management. Leadership supplies vision, direction and commitment; management makes sure that things actually happen (the chairman and chief executive of a company will often find themselves fulfilling these respective roles). Depending on the organization in question this balance will be oriented more one way than the other. The rather obvious point to make, though, is that both are needed: an organization in which everyone is committed to an undeliverable ideal will not tend to be too successful (with the exception of the occasional political party); but neither will an organization which is very efficient at doing the wrong things.

So why is leadership important to management developers and trainers? The first point is that training and development activities need to be undertaken within a framework which gives direction. Without the ideological and business alignment that true leadership brings, training is of at most peripheral use, and becomes training for training's sake. It is no coincidence that organizations which are managed rather than led will often cut their training budgets first in recessionary times, while more visionary organizations invest in training and developing their people to enable them to deliver the organizational vision.

At a more fundamental level, leadership binds people together in a common purpose – an absolutely essential process for all organizations. The organization itself may have only one leader, but the development of a 'leadership culture' in which individual work units are led rather than managed, and in which leaders of the future are identified and developed like queen bee larvae, requires training in the fundamentals of leadership. Whether or not a leader can be made rather than born is a debatable point, but the culture can be encouraged and developed through career guidance and skills workshops.

In the wider world beyond the organization, leadership is coming under the microscope. It has been suggested that the price being paid for contemporary economic systems is far too high: much of our individual gains from a higher standard of living become tied up in defensive or positional spending: defensive because we need to spend more money to protect ourselves from pollution or crime; positional because we have to spend more and more to get less and less (when everyone can afford a car, road travel becomes a nightmare, so the rich get helicopters, and when everyone has a helicopter then ...). The white heat of technology has failed to deliver the promised leisure time we would all have to be trained to enjoy: instead, people whose jobs have been robbed by microprocessors have enforced leisure time with no money to enjoy it, while those that are left seem to be working longer and longer hours. And those who lead seem powerless to do anything about this, citing external forces beyond their control.

But true leadership is precisely about enabling people to feel a sense of control over their destiny and taking the group forwards in a direction that is best for all. True leadership does not give in to a passive acceptance of fate but empowers and creates, bringing a sparkle to life in whatever activities it is concerned with. From the point of view both of individual needs and of taking organizations and society forward in a positive frame of mind, leadership – or the lack of it – is the critical issue of our time.

In this chapter we look at several alternative views on leadership and their implications for management development. The first section looks at the work of Norman Dixon, who has written extensively about military leaders and their driving motivations. We then examine the myth of the hero – the journey that mythical heroes went through in order to become true leaders. Finally we look at Zen, and what leaders can learn from its approaches.

THE PSYCHOLOGY OF LEADERSHIP

In his book *On the Psychology of Military Incompetence*, Norman Dixon analyses some of the worst cases of hopeless stupidity perpetrated by British commanders. He isolates 14 characteristics based on military leadership practices in the Boer War, the seige of Kut, and the use of tanks in the First World War. While there are obvious differences between the organization of the military and the culture of a business organization, there are also some startling differences. To translate Dixon's characteristics into applications for industry today we have reduced the 14 characteristics to 10:

- Lack of information-gathering networks.

- Ignoring information which does not fit with preconceptions.

- Underestimating competitors.

- Indecisiveness in decision making and action – no clear vision.

- Lack of innovation and investment in new technology.

- Lack of radical thought or action – reliance on past methods.

- Refusing to take responsibility for mistakes and blaming others.

- Wasting effort and resources.

- Ignoring needs of employees.

- Trusting to luck or fate.

This list of characteristics is echoed in the works of management theorists who concentrate on business. Jim Butler, for example, in a paper entitled 'Learning Skills for Strategic Change' (see 'Further Reading' for details), gives case examples of managers' inability to learn from experience and the efforts they put into becoming 'skilled incompetents' – people who are clever at not learning the skills needed to move the organization forward.

CLINGING TO STABILITY

Why do managers stick to tried and trusted ways of doing things, even when they are patently absurd? Dixon talks about the human need to reduce anxiety by making the world a stable, unsurprising place. We see this in the military in its clearly defined rules and procedures, the rigid application of 'bull' to stop questioning or independent thought. We see it everywhere in a 'better the devil you know' outlook, and in a fear of the unknown (often expressed as blind prejudice based on ignorance). And we personally have seen it in the workplace in several memorable examples: the operations director of a large retail chain flying into a rage because every store in the UK did not have its toothpaste counter laid out in exactly the same way;

or managers of forty years' experience breaking down in tears when a woman boss was appointed.

Fortunately, however, Dixon also provides a list of what he sees as the characteristics of good leaders. The good military commanders in his study had high achievement needs in terms of improving their own professional skills (whereas the bad ones wanted simply to promote their own self-aggrandizement). Other positive characteristics were:

- A better memory for uncompleted tasks and predisposition to task completion.

- A preference when choosing working partners for successful strangers rather than unsuccessful friends.

- A greater activity in the community of which they are a part.

Dixon closes by quoting Erik Erikson on two key requirements for good leaders:

1. *Purpose* the courage to envisage and pursue valued goals uninhibited by the defeat of infantile fantasies, by guilt and by the inhibiting fear of punishment

2. *Wisdom* a detached concern with life itself, in the fear of death itself.

BROADENING OUT

Wellington and Napoleon are both examples of leaders who displayed the positive qualities cited by Dixon. He gives examples of Wellington taking full responsibility for military errors, refusing to sacrifice his men unnecessarily, even crying on the battlefield because of the loss of so many of his men. He was open to new ideas, took infinite care in his military planning and could be detached and witty. Napoleon was equally concerned for his people: he offered 'a career open to talent . . . so as to provide that no citizen, however humble, should be barred from highest office'. He had a wide range of intellectual interests and was open and generous. Certainly Wellington and Napoleon both provided clear vision and direction and gained the full commitment of their men by their values and behaviour.

What emerges from many of these positive examples is a picture of a successful leader as someone who accepts the full responsibilities of his or her role when on the job, but who seeks to broaden his or her horizons when off the job. This is backed up by the writing of John Kotter (see 'Further Reading') who found that effective chief executives in the United States were distinguished from less effective CEOs by their interests in the world outside business: in other words they had both depth and breadth. The implications of this are that aspiring leaders need to take an interest in self development, be unconcerned about admitting mistakes and be genuinely concerned to do better. Good news for all management developers: find your true leaders and they will keep coming back to you!

WHAT'S DRIVING YOU?

Perhaps the hardest skill to be learned in the self-development process required of the leader is the ability to admit weakness, to overcome our childhood need for approval. A lot of work on this theme has been done in the area of transactional analysis (TA), an approach to psychotherapy developed in the USA by Dr Eric Berne. One of the central ideas of TA is the concept of 'life scripts': these are the scripts by which we act out our lives, laid down in childhood. The scripts are governed by 'drivers', parental admonitions which we take on board and use to run our lives without being consciously aware of the fact. There are five identified drivers. The first, *'Be strong'* is probably the driver for many of the inept military leaders researched by Dixon, and has a resonance for anyone who feels unable to show weakness and always to stay in control. The other four drivers are: *'Be perfect'*; *'Hurry up'*; *'Please others'*; and *'Try hard'*.

In TA, once a primary driver has been established, the patterns of behaviour which it produces can be tackled and adjusted through the process of psychotherapy.

There is really no excuse for bad or missing leadership, once you know what to avoid. As the inescapable truth seems to be that most of what you need to avoid lies within you, only you can identify the work that needs to be done to address it. But the first – and major – step is to admit that there is actually work to be done.

QUESTIONS

- Are you a leader or a manager? (Both are fine, as long as you are clear about which you prefer.)

- What is your vision for your own life? For work? Why do you need one?

- Who do you admire most as a leader and why?

- What positive characteristics do the good leaders you know share with those suggested by Norman Dixon?

- What characteristics do the bad leaders you know have in common with Dixon's list?

- What is needed most from leaders in your particular organization?

- What drivers do the leaders or managers you know exhibit?

- What are your drivers?

- What can (or should) you do about them?

- In the light of Dixon's analysis, how would you develop leaders within your own organization?

TRAINING AND DEVELOPMENT GUIDELINES

In terms of developing the *skills* of leadership, a starting point for the trainer could be the 'bad leader' characteristics that Norman Dixon gives. These can be used as the basis for identifying the skills that individuals need to develop if they are to avoid these mistakes. It may also be worth exploring the possibility of using exercises or structured interview techniques to help people understand their 'drivers' and how these may affect their leadership skills. 'Upward feedback' – in which individuals are evaluated by those they lead on a selection of leadership practices – can be a highly effective method of developing the openness about personal weakness that characterizes effective leaders.

However, the most effective way of developing leadership skills would seem to be experience, most of which will come from work itself. On training programmes the opportunity to provide pure experience – as opposed to abstract concepts – of leadership skills is limited, since by their very nature they require a certain number of followers to make the process realistic. It is possible, though, to set up intricate exercises which demand that the leader manage complicated information, tasks and people against a background of uncertainty. Trainers who use the outdoors to positively develop these skills can find that participants become completely absorbed in 24-hour exercises that contain a series of difficult and challenging decision points. It is by observing real leadership in action and giving feedback on observable leadership practices (whether derived from Dixon's list or others) that participants have a real opportunity to improve their leadership skills.

The challenge for trainers is that this type of activity will also stretch and challenge them – since they will not be as in control as they might be in a classroom environment. The key training skills in leadership development are much more to do with accurate process observation and giving back feedback that is developmental and relevant.

LEADERSHIP AND SELF-DEVELOPMENT

For thousands of years, people throughout the world have used myths to reassure themselves that they are not alone in the kinds of experiences they have. Myths are stories that we can use to understand how our personal lives resonate with, and correspond to, universal patterns. When we identify with some aspect of a particular myth, we are tapping into the combined energies of all those before us who have reacted in the same way. We experience the vital essence of those involved in the stories. If they are gods and goddesses, as in Greek mythology for example, then we draw strength from the magnitude of their experience, just as the Greeks found catharsis in these stories of heroism and tragedy.

Most myths deal extensively with leaders – or certainly with heroes and heroines of some kind – and contain themes which are present in the lives of many managers and executives. Joseph Campbell, who spent a great deal of his life collecting myths from around the world, identified certain crucial phases in the journey that the heroes of myths underwent:

1. An *awareness* of some kind of lack in his or her own life.

2. A *rejection* of the life he or she is currently leading, and an alienation from the society of which he or she is a part.

3. A *journey* which involves hardship and suffering on a quest to find the unknown missing aspect of the hero's life – be it a search for meaning, understanding, power or love. This

journey may involve a battle against tremendous odds, including a battle for his or her own life; or it may be a journey through a barren wilderness without nourishment.

4. If the hero completes the journey, he or she gains inner strength, wisdom and power, and is ready to move on the *gaining of the prize* – whatever that may be.

5. He or she then *returns* to where the journey began, bearing his or her newfound wisdom, and using this new gift for the benefit of those left behind.

An example of such a myth from British culture is the story of King Arthur, who with the knights of the Round Table set out to attain a vision of heaven on earth through a search for the Holy Grail – the chalice that was supposed to contain Christ's blood. Most of the knights perished along the way – in trying to become more pure and holy, their quest ended in heaven – while those that remained acted as guides towards living a more spiritual and meaningful life.

This may appear rather divorced from the day-to-day life of the average workplace, but when senior and successful managers are interviewed about their careers the same themes and patterns are found. They have a determination to better themselves, to move beyond and above where they started – to find the missing piece, if you like – and to make a difference. They may face difficulties because of their determination to stand up for what they believe, even if this means being cast into the wilderness. If they complete their journey, however, they return to the fold bringing their newfound skills, knowledge and depth with them – along with a belief in themselves and an awareness of their strengths and weaknesses.

Often, however, those leaders that we have are not paragons of virtue. They have not developed as they need to, and organizations (and nations) suffer as a result. Leaders who seek power for its own sake may find themselves in such a scenario. One myth which has relevance for this type of leader is the story of Wotan, as told in Wagner's *Ring* cycle. (Apologies to those who admire this opera's complexity, as we condense 17½ hours into two paragraphs.)

Wotan, a ruler and leader, has got to where he is by making deals with enemies and friends alike, binding them by constraints, enhancing constantly his own power, and building monuments to himself (the castle at Valhalla). This has become a way of life for him, and in the quest of power he is prepared to sacrifice his family's needs. As the story continues, Wotan becomes more and more aware of the trap he has built for himself and how, because of his mutual commitments, he has little room for manoeuvre. In building power networks, he has become impotent.

His way out is to try to get his son to act independently of him, but still to do the things Wotan wants done. This represents the beginnings of an attempt to escape from the confines of power while still trying to cling on to it – power without responsibility. When he finds that he can't evade his responsibilities he reverts to sheer exercise of power – even though it causes him pain. It is only when a truly independent person defies him and breaks his power that Wotan accepts he can't control everything and has failed in that attempt.

Leaders and managers who try and gain power without accepting their moral responsibilities display a lack of concern for people and their welfare which one would never see in a true king-ruler or hero. King Arthur insisted that no one – not even himself – was above the law, and he strove to lead the country for the benefit of its people.

Charles Handy drew on myths and legends in his book *Gods of Management*. He asks managers to identify themselves with one of four Greek gods:

Zeus: operates on power relationships (similar to Wotan);
Apollo: wants order, certainty and stability;
Athena: wants to achieve, to do things well;
Dionysus: lives for pleasure.

Most managers, when encouraged, can find illumination in the process of identification with one of these archetypes. The benefits of this process, as we mentioned earlier, lie in individuals finding metaphors and frameworks to help them identify positive and negative qualities in themselves.

The ancient Greeks used their own myths as the centrepiece of their tragedies – major theatrical events which dealt with issues of power and authority. The central themes of tragedy – often centring around power, jealousy or greed – are just as recognizable today, and many of the forces at work in tragedy are responsible for the downfall of many modern leaders: *hubris*, for example, which represents overweening ambition likely to lead to a fall from grace (in the sense of pride coming before a fall); or *anagnorisis* and *peripeteia*, the combination of a tragic mistake which engenders the hero's loss of fortune, and the hero (or leader's) own recognition of that. And how many of us have been on the receiving end of some *nemesis* (divine retribution) at one time or another?

Myths can be used as metaphors to free the imagination and give more depth to our working lives. A daily commute on the train becomes far more rewarding if you see the similarities to Ulysses on his journeys around the Mediterranean, or see yourself pitting your wits against the vast body of other commuters like David squaring up to Goliath.

QUESTIONS

- Think of the stories, legends, myths that you know. Which one represents your personal story?

- Which character, god or goddess would you say you were most like – and why?

- What are their (and your) strengths – and possible weaknesses?

- At which stage in the story are you? What's the likely outcome?

- Which gods or goddesses, in which stories, can you recognize in your friends or colleagues?

- What lessons would you recognize as being necessary for you to take from your chosen myth or story?

TRAINING AND DEVELOPMENT GUIDELINES

Myths can be a useful way into a particular topic: most people recognize the stories, even if they don't know all the details; myths tend to portray universal truths, so they can be adapted to fit many recognizable management situations; and they get you out of the day-to-day work arena and open up the possibilities for tackling your chosen issue(s).

Encouraging individuals to use myths to tell their own stories can be very useful too: most people are either reticent in revealing details about themselves and their attitudes to work, or simply do not have a framework to articulate whatever is at the heart of their management style. By getting managers to identify with a particular myth – even to invent one if a suitable one doesn't exist – you start a process of storytelling which allows individuals to tell personal stories in a non-threatening, almost anonymous way.

Language is a vital area in which the trainer should be fluent and highly skilled. Language is at the heart of story telling and myth: the trainer can, and should, use his or her own grasp of words to help people retell their own stories. If this all sounds rather esoteric, it is in many ways little different from the training process itself. For example, many people believe that they have no skills in a particular area, perhaps because of the way a subject was taught at school, or because of feedback they have had from others. They have a 'myth' that they are useless at, say, maths. The good trainer can get them to retell their story so they discover that, taught in a different way, they may well develop the skills they believe they can never have.

All training is about this changing of viewpoints, beliefs and perspectives: good training changes – or at least questions and adjusts – the world-view of participants. 'Myth reading' is about understanding how people define their worlds and helping them change these definitions as appropriate. The key training skills are the ability to listen fully to all that is being said (and not being said) and to use words to help these changes.

ZEN AND THE ART OF LEADERSHIP

Why should management developers and trainers be concerned with an oriental religion or philosophy? What does a discipline based partly on the Taoists (of whom more later) and on the sayings of Confucius, both from ancient China, have to say to the modern manager?

There is a story about the scholar who went to a Zen monk for knowledge. As he continued to ask the monk question after question, to which he received no reply, the monk poured out a cup of tea for him, but carried on pouring and pouring even when the cup was full. Eventually the scholar protested that the tea was overflowing the cup and on to the table. 'So it is with your mind,' said the monk. 'How can you learn wisdom until you empty your mind of all the assumptions that are in it already?'

In the context of management and leadership, the assumptions which fill our brains are beliefs about the way managers should act; about what is 'right' or professional. ('Being professional,' a colleague once observed, 'is often just an excuse to be a bastard.') Such assumptions are often to do with following what the organization thinks (or what we think the organization thinks) is the right way, with maintaining the status quo. What Zen teaches is that these assumptions – our 'mindset' if you like – block our natural effectiveness and get in the way of true competence. Zen tells us that we have to learn not to strive to do the right thing, but just to do, while emptying our minds as we empty the cup.

There are several sports-training methods which use this kind of approach, in which sportsmen and women are encouraged to stop trying, to stop measuring themselves against imaginary standards, and simply to play tennis, or golf, or whatever. Those who try this technique find that their skills do improve – it certainly worked for the Samurai warriors, whose abilities in swordsmanship and archery were the best in the world. Those who practise the Alexander technique as a relaxation discipline will also be familiar with this principle (see Chapter 5 for more on Alexander, in the context of coaching).

DOING WHAT COMES NATURALLY

Being natural is a key element in Zen and is equally applicable to leadership:

> Ruling is strengthening. If you lead along a straight road, who will dare go by a crooked one?

or:

> The way out is through the open door. Why is it that no one will use it?

Listening to managers (or anyone else for that matter) discussing their problems, we often find that the solutions (the open doors) seem obvious to us. But when we are in difficulties we too have problems with seeing the obvious, because of all the assumptions and beliefs our minds hold. Readers familiar with the work of Edward de Bono may notice a relationship between his concept of lateral thinking and the Zen approach to getting away from traditional assumptions (what de Bono calls 'tethering factors'). It was also de Bono who said 'The need to be right all the time is the biggest bar there is to new ideas', a Zen statement if ever there was one.

BE AWARE

Another essential aspect of Zen is awareness, which in this context means taking all factors into account – not as part of a systematic, logical process, but in the sense of being instantaneously aware and alert to all that is happening:

> To hear the unheard is a necessary discipline to be a good ruler; for only when a ruler has learned to listen closely to the people's hearts, hearing their feelings uncommunicated, pains unexpressed and complaints not spoken of, can he hope to inspire confidence in his people, understand when something is wrong, and meet the true needs of his citizens. (Chan Kim, W and Manborgne R A (1992) 'Parables of Leadership', *Harvard Business Review* (July-August.)

To hear the unheard, it is necessary to operate, as we have said, without assumptions, with openness and humility. 'I am their leader, therefore I follow them' is a good axiom. This is what led Jan Carlzon, CEO of the Swedish national airline SAS, to spend large amounts of time listening to what his employees had to say before he formulated his vision for the organization; it is why many Japanese organizations (if the Japanese are allowed to practise Zen) spend apparently inordinate amounts of time on consultation before implementing organizational change – and manage the change quickly and with virtually no resistance.

FIND SPACE

The elements of Zen all reinforce one another: the mind is left out of the process, which leads to a naturalness and openness to the moment, which leads to a need for space. The need to fill each waking moment with busy activity (have you ever reflected on the etymological significance of the word *'business'*?) is completely at odds with Zen teaching, which emphasizes the need to allow space for contemplation, for things to work. With total communication in an organization, for example, it would grind to a halt as there would be no space left for people to think or do anything (how many people in your office complain about being swamped with memos or other bits of information?). Space and emptiness, says Zen, allows noise to become music; space is needed between words so that we can read them. Emptiness and space are crucial to all we do and the wise leader allows people space to open up, to express their thoughts, to develop ideas and action.

As the modern business environment shrinks the timescales within which things can be done (with fax and modem allowing instant communication of data, so leading to tighter deadlines for projects) there is less and less space for people to express themselves. A need has been seen for organizations to move away from concentrating exclusively on tasks that are urgent and important to tasks that are important but not urgent; and in the process finding some space in their schedules for creating excellence of output – something which urgency often denies us. This is a concrete expression of the truth within the principles of Zen.

Zen also warns against too much intellectualization, teaching instead of the need to experience, to *do*, to fully appreciate what reality is all about. It is quite easy, surrounded by modern technology, to divorce oneself from reality. People become employees or simply 'the workforce', and are represented in many executives' reality as little more than a fixed (or perhaps at least semi-variable in more recent times) overhead.

Once you intellectualize and objectify others, then a little humanity is lost in you. The world becomes instead a series of complex transactions based on gain considerations, and the quality of life goes down. Why should a shop assistant smile and say a sincere 'good morning' if he or she is being treated mechanically by those further up the chain? And Zen is nothing if it is not about humanity and about the quality of each and every transaction, in which we do our utmost to give of our best. In Japanese industry this is expressed as *dantotsu* – being the best of the best, continuously improving. It applies equally well to relationships between people and to the making of goods; and, as we have already observed, leaders more than anyone have a continuous need to improve themselves, to be the best in a way that is natural and not based on assumptions.

Finally, Zen is about savouring the present moment, expressing joy and pleasure through an awareness of what happens in everyday life – and finding a unique personal meaning in the way that our lives flow like rivers along their different courses. Ultimately, however, as with many contemporary management philosophies, the main trick is not to take things too seriously. After all:

> Sometimes one is up
>   and sometimes one is down
> therefore the wise man avoids
>   excesses and complacency.

And because avoiding excess is as crucial to authors of books on management as to anyone else, enough on Zen.

> It is a pleasure
>   when a follower thinks of
>   something I didn't know,
> It is warming when a customer
>   reminds me unexpectedly
>   of a small favour we did them
> It is delightful when our team
>   comes up with ideas that
>   we share,
> It is wonderful when we are
>   surprised by superb performance
> And it is so good
>   to forget about work
>   on the way home.

QUESTIONS

- What is it you don't need to know, that you could empty your mind of?

- What is not being said, that you need to hear?

- Where are the spaces in your work and life?

- What are the 'open doors' to issues in your life?

- What do you need to just *do*?

TRAINING AND DEVELOPMENT GUIDELINES

Zen cannot be taught: it is about allowing a process to happen. The only way that participants on training programmes can absorb Zen messages is from the example of the trainer. So as a trainer, if you are interested in this area, you need to practise the concepts yourself. This means being natural and allowing and accepting what happens without attempting to judge whether events are right or wrong. This, of course, is exactly the opposite of what trainers are normally expected to do, which is to show the 'right way' of a particular style of management.

The way past this dilemma is to understand that often the trainer must set guidelines without suggesting one right way, or becoming caught up in a sense of his or her own superiority. There is an Edward de Bono exercise in which participants are asked to choose the odd one out from five different geometric figures and told – with some emphasis – to be certain they get the right answer. In fact all the figures are equally different, but whatever answer each participant gives is rewarded by the trainer with 'Well done, you are absolutely right.' At first this produces confusion and often resentment, because people feel they are not getting the right answer. They may also be anxious about impressing the others with their unique knowledge, or be frightened of being seen to get it wrong. Then gradually people come to see that being 'right' is a function of the rules and assumptions you start with (this is a theme to which we will return regularly in these pages).

The consequence is that trainer and participants can relate as equals pooling their respective knowledge and discussing and exploring issues and problems instead of being over-concerned with getting the right answer, which would ultimately, within this context, hinder their development. Such an opening out and broadening of horizons is what most trainers aim for.

The true Zen trainer will develop appropriate process skills: being aware of what is happening in the training arena, of the blockages to learning, and above all enjoying the activity of training. A vital skill is allowing participants the space to reflect and absorb what is being delivered. There is often pressure on trainers to deliver more and more in less and less time. Needless to say the end result of such a tendency is that participants are swamped by knowledge and skills development: they have no time to review, to pause and understand what all this means to them. Their minds are like the cup of tea into which more and more is being poured.

Finally, Zen emphasizes a sense of play and fun. A Zen trainer (and there are many who fit this description without knowing anything about Zen) will enjoy, and learn from, the participants' comments and reactions. As trainers our minds have to be empty in order to be receptive to what participants think and feel. A true Zen trainer would be prepared to throw away an entire programme in order to be truly responsive to participants' needs. Before you throw away your schedules and learning objectives, however, the essence of this is to highlight the importance of true dialogue between trainer and participants. One of the best trainers we know describes his training events as conversations – but conversations with clear learning outcomes.

FURTHER READING

Leadership is a vast topic, and the amount of management literature on the subject is correspondingly vast. Accordingly, we have limited this guide to books or articles which follow similar lines of thought to this chapter.

The very best book on leadership (including the lack of it) is that by Dixon, N (1976) *On the Psychology of Military Incompetence*, Futura. An in-depth, scholarly, but highly entertaining and readable account of what is necessary for leadership, it should be read by all those who have any connection whatsoever with leading others. Some of its themes are reflected in Butler, J (1992) 'Learning Skills for Strategic Change', *Journal of Strategic Change*, Vol 1. This is an excellent article on the difficulties that senior managers have in stepping outside their own narrow frames of reference. Kotter, J P (1990) 'What Leaders really Do', *Harvard Business Review*, May-June, examines the distinction between leadership and management, and argues the case for thinking about leaders not as people only at the top of organizations.

Books on the journey that the hero or leader undertakes are usually more rarefied than those on leadership itself. Probably the best overall is Campbell, J (1988) *The Power of Myth*, Doubleday. This is a book which roams over a vast territory of ideas and speculations and which has enormous implications for the way in which we all view the myths of our own lives, and for what we can do to influence our own individual journeys. A more practical guide to achieving this is Pearson, Carol S (1991) *Awakening the Heroes Within*, Harper (San Francisco). Carol Pearson gives detailed exercises for determining the stages that each of us has reached in terms of our personal journey, and includes a questionnaire to help identify which myth is most relevant to the individual reader.

Bolen, J S (1992) *Ring of Power: The Abandoned Child, the Authoritarian Father and the Disembodied Feminine*, Harper (San Francisco), is much more focused on the abuses of power and the betrayal of moral principles in the search for and attempt to retain this power. The book is an analysis of Wagner's *Ring* cycle, but the message is the same as that of Dixon, Butler and Kotter: don't be limited by your own views but be ready to explore and develop. Bly, R (1990) *Iron John: A Book About Men*, Addison-Wesley, is worth reading even by those who back away from the much-satirized movement it spawned, as it draws some interesting conclusions around the links between modern industrial man and his mythological predecessors. It also offers another perspective on the journey of life and development – but probably won't help female leaders very much. The most directly management-oriented of the references in the chapter is Handy, C (1978), *Gods of Management*, Souvenir Press.

In terms of Zen and its relation with leadership it is probably best to read books on Zen generally and apply the principles yourself. Unfortunately Zen authors tell us it is impossible to describe Zen, so the process is in danger of becoming a thankless task. If you get nowhere and want a shortcut, try Radha (1990) *The Zen Way to be an Effective Manager*, Mercury Business.

CHAPTER 4

Communication and Teamwork

4 COMMUNICATION AND TEAMWORK

INTRODUCTION

As we have noted elsewhere in this book, the focus of organizations in the nineties seems to be moving more and more to the importance of people as individuals. The cynic will tell you that this is because the organizations in question have shed so many of their staff that they need to keep the remainder happy in order to get as much as possible out of them. Whatever the reason, the way that individuals relate to each other – their communication or interpersonal skills – is increasingly coming under the microscope.

The importance of face-to-face relationships works on a number of levels. First, there are contemporary management theories which emphasize the quality of the relationship between manager and subordinate – not only in terms of coaching (see Chapter 5) but also in terms of being able to manage the quality of the employee's performance in a climate of trust and clarity about shared objectives.

Then there are those organizations which rely on the concept of 'alignment' – that is, there are few if any formal hierarchies and employees 'fall into line' by virtue of their shared commitment to a brilliantly communicated organizational vision. In these organizations, it is again the quality of the interpersonal relationships which can set the seal on this rather utopian scenario.

Finally, there is the simple fact that an organization – any kind of organization – in which people communicate freely, openly and *honestly* with each other is likely to have its wheels well oiled, as it were. We are back to that word 'climate' again: the climate of an organization is very simply how it 'feels' to work there. Many organizations have climates of mistrust and secrecy

– and it is at the basic interpersonal level that such climates are reinforced. But that need not be the end of the story. We looked in Chapter 2 at the idea of the organization which advances and develops by means of its peripheral norms being breached: it is through changes in the quality of communication at the level of the individual that such mighty climates can be changed.

The changing, flattening structures of modern organizations have also given rise to a renewed interest in the power of team-working as a way of achieving results. This has come about partly because of the emphasis placed by continuous improvement techniques on the importance of the 'cross-functional team', but also because of a recognititon that a healthy team is essentially synergistic – it produces results which are more than the sum of its parts.

There are many ways of looking at and analysing teams: in terms of structure, roles, performance, results, and many more. We concentrate in this chapter on the interpersonal dynamics operating within teams, as a natural progression from looking at the way in which individuals communicate and behave with each other. Most of the material, though, is written from the perspective of the individual operating in terms of interpersonal behaviour. The learning can then be applied to face-to-face communication or to teamwork, whichever is appropriate.

We will look first at the dynamics which appear to govern the way any two people behave with each other, focusing on how we shadow each other – not in terms of mirroring, but in terms of finding opposite standpoints and aspects. We then take a whistle-stop tour through some theatrical techniques and apply them to improving interpersonal and team effectiveness. Finally we take a behavioural model of interpersonal behaviour and use it to look at the things that get in the way of teams performing effectively.

UNWRITTEN LAWS OF INTERPERSONAL COMMUNICATION

For every action there is an equal and opposite reaction
Newton's Third Law

Carl Jung, whose concepts of life development we looked at in Chapter 2, was very keen, as we saw, on the idea of the shadow

– that part of ourselves which is everything that our conscious self is not. The image conjured up is of each of us, going through life being shadowed – literally – by an alter ego who behaves in a way that is always the opposite of our own.

We don't have to look within ourselves, however, to see this dynamic at work. Many couples will testify to the frequent experience of one partner becoming more positive in outlook when the other partner is depressed; of one partner taking a submissive role when the other behaves in a dominant fashion; one partner being strong for the other in a time of crisis.

One can see this same dynamic operating in offices up and down the country any day of the year. One example will serve: we did some work for the finance director of a large electronics firm. He was a pleasant enough person, but he tyrannized his secretarial staff beyond the point of endurance – or so they told us. What actually seemed to be happening was that, before he ever had a chance to give them a task, they would each take a submissive posture, whether by apologizing for something he hadn't yet complained about, or by speaking in hushed tones as if afraid some nemesis might befall them. Our finance director responded by exhibiting dominant behaviour – by being task-focused, almost dictatorial, and by losing patience with any slight deviation from what was requested.

The director and the secretarial team had locked each other into a vicious circle. Doubtless there must have been some first cause, an occasion on which his behaviour caused them to react. But the situation at the point we saw it was one in which his behaviour was being reinforced as 'correct' by the behaviour of his staff: they walked around wearing signs saying 'kick me', and all he was doing was obeying.

The most interesting thing happened on our last day. One of the secretaries was ill, and had been replaced by a temp. Temporary staff, of course, can be notorious in their disrespect for authority – they, after all, can walk out of the company and leave others to pick up the pieces. This particular temp very simply took no nonsense from the finance director: if he asked her to do something she considered unreasonable (as he was wont to do, if only because the other secretaries were so terrified of him they would always agree) she told him no. Did fire and brimstone rain down upon her head? In fact he rang her agency and asked whether she was available permanently. His relief that someone at long last had stopped playing his shadow and had met him on equal terms was tangible.

There may be many benefits in taking an opposite stance to the person with whom you are dealing: but relying on this 'shadow dynamic' can often reduce interpersonal communication to an unproductive game of ping-pong in which we concentrate not on the other person's message, but on the tone in which they present it. And it is the tone which can get in the way: this is worth examining further.

THE HOSTILITY/PARANOIA DYNAMIC

Much of the interpersonal communication that goes on in the average office is founded on two undesirable aspects of personality: hostility and paranoia. If we think of communication skills as either expressive (giving out information – speaking) or receptive (taking in information – listening) then we see the two aspects working as follows:

* Expressive communication:

  Hostility says 'The only opinions which count are mine.'

  Paranoia says 'I'm sure you think I'm an idiot for saying this, but...'

* Receptive communication:

  Hostility says 'As soon as this idiot shuts up I can talk about what I want to talk about.'

  Paranoia says 'Why are you talking to me about this? What do I know? What will I have to do in return?'

We can also think of this kind of dynamic as aggression/submission, but hostility/paranoia captures the flavour of the way many of us travel through life: they are essentially lonely pursuits. Those of us who travel to work see hostility in action on a daily basis, in the impotent rage of commuters in traffic jams or on crowded trains. These individuals seek an outlet for their battle against the world ('How dare the world/God/whoever make me suffer like this') and so spend their working days looking for outlets for this pent-up hostility. Other individuals who suffer the same feeling of everything being stacked against them blame themselves ('Why does everything happen to me?')

and spend their days in a wash of paranoia, constantly seeking confirmation of their lowly status.

Anyone taking either of these standpoints will tend to find themselves seeking out individuals with the opposite style in order to reconfirm their own position. Thus our finance director became more hostile as his secretaries became more paranoid – and vice versa. Most of us lack the unshakeable self-confidence required to stand up to someone behaving in a dominant way; likewise, someone behaving submissively represents too great a temptation for most would-be dominators to resist. This is essentially how the shadow dynamic perpetuates itself.

FINDING AN EQUILIBRIUM

Dr Eric Berne, who developed the model of transactional analysis which is being increasingly applied to management development, summarized hostility/aggression as taking the standpoint 'I'm OK–You're not OK'; in other words, I will seek to dominate others and not take them seriously. Submission/paranoia, on the other hand, takes the standpoint 'I'm not OK–You're OK'; in other words, other people know better than me, and are more capable.

Berne's message is that true interpersonal effectiveness requires the standpoint 'I'm OK–You're OK'; in other words, if you want to be like you are, that's fine: it's no skin off my nose, and provided I am able to be myself in return, we can co-exist perfectly well. This rather alarmingly laid-back outlook is in fact remarkably effective in a workplace setting. Respecting others' unique and individual personalities – whether we actually like them as people or not – in return for being allowed to be unique ourselves implies that all communication taking place is actually being listened to.

It is important to remember that mutual respect – which is the easiest way of summarizing this concept – does not mean not getting your own way: that would be submission. On the other hand, it certainly does not mean getting your own way at the expense of others. Working in a true attitude of mutual respect means, as far as possible, that everyone gets their own way. It is the basis of most successful negotiation techniques (where it goes under the *nom de voyage* 'win–win'), and implies that provided we acknowledge another person's standpoint they are far more likely to accept ours (think of customer service techniques, where dealing with an angry customer first involves acknowledging his or her right to be angry if he/she wants to – 'Obviously you're upset about this'/'I can see you feel strongly about this' – before going on to tackle objective issues of whether the complaint is justifiable).

IMPLICATIONS FOR COMMUNICATION

The objective of anyone considering the lessons of this topic must be to find the middle line – the 'I'm OK–You're OK' standpoint. This means developing an awareness of the presence of hostility/aggression and paranoia/submission in yourself and in others. There are two main 'don'ts' when dealing with others using this model:

1. Don't take the 'shadow position'. That is, if someone appears to be taking a dominant, aggressive or hostile position in their face-to-face dealings with you, then don't allow yourself to retreat into a submissive or paranoid mode of operating: it will make them more extreme and you more defeated and miserable. Similarly, if someone else is behaving in a submissive way, resist the temptation to be dominant or aggressive – it will reinforce their behaviour and give them a subliminal justification for continuing.

2. Having said all that, don't match like with like. It is equally counterproductive to take an aggressive line with someone who is behaving aggressively: it might make you feel better for a few seconds, but you may get your nose broken. And two people relating to each other with both taking a submissive standpoint will pull each other down a relentlessly miserable spiral, until they reach the mutual position: 'I'm not OK, neither are you, what's the point in carrying on?'

What is needed is for you, as someone displaying support for the standpoint of mutual respect, simply (but of course it isn't *that* simple!) to stand your ground somewhere in the middle. Meeting aggression with calm certainty, while acknowledging the reality of the other person's aggression, will start to bring him or her in to meet you. The same stance taken with someone behaving submissively is likely to transfer some of your calm confidence to them: you are being strong *without* being threatening, and it is this which will win you an equal hearing.

Anyone working in teams will see the obvious benefits of purging the shadow dynamic from the team process. Any team member with excessive doses of hostility is likely to incite paranoic reactions in some, if not all, team members. Two or more hostile or aggressive team members will display the unproductive 'like vs like' behaviour described above. Submissive team members will incite aggression – or at the very least irritation – from others, and two or more together may well get stuck in the kind of 'No, you go first' routine which is anathema to truly assertive and respectful team behaviour.

QUESTIONS

- How do you deal with aggression in others? (Do you fight fire with fire, tell them to 'calm down', or acknowledge the strength of their feelings before attempting to find the truth?)

- How do you deal with submissiveness in others? (Do you apologize for bothering them, tell them to 'pull themselves together', or find a way of reassuring them that they have equal status in the transaction?)

- Is there a climate of hostility among managers in your organization? If so, how do subordinates react to this?

- Are you frightened of your boss? If so, why? Could you see yourself getting your own way with him/her?

- How do your subordinates treat you (and you them)? Respectfully? Aggressively? With over-familiarity?

- What happens in teams of which you are a member? Do some members use the team as a vehicle for their hostility or paranoia?

TRAINING AND DEVELOPMENT GUIDELINES

Communication skills training is, or should be, in every trainer's set of competencies. And yet there are probably times when we catch ourselves not putting into practice what we preach. It is at these times that the 'shadow dynamic' of communication is at work: we are being hooked into others' projections or paranoia. For trainers themselves the implications are manifold as we deal with people all the time in the training role, and it is all too easy to find ourselves being trapped by these interpersonal dynamics.

Trainers therefore have little choice but to try and overcome any tendency to be caught by these dramas, whether it is a regular show of sardonic wit by one particular group member, outright hostility, or the participant who prefaces every presentation of the results of an exercise with 'This is going to be a load of rubbish . . .' or similar. Many trainers will respond to challenges in the classroom by taking either an 'I'm not OK–You're OK' stance ('Yes, you're absolutely right, the theory is flawed, I'll go and redesign the session') or, more often, 'I'm OK–You're not OK' ('What the hell do you know? Are you a management trainer?') This attitude gets in the way of true communication which, as Eric Berne explained, only happens when all parties to a discussion have a genuine 'I'm OK–You're OK' standpoint. (Trainers often have another variant: 'I'm almost OK–You're almost OK – we'll all be fine after we've had our training.')

These kinds of dynamic are also the starting point for training activities. Of course, basic expressive and receptive skills must be taught, but they will be useless if the participant is stuck in the belief that he or she is too superior or inferior to communicate with certain people. In training, as in any other endeavour, skills are only effective if built upon a foundation of motivation to use those skills.

REHEARSAL & SPONTANEITY

The ancient Greeks used their form of theatre – Tragedy – as a catalyst for a process of catharsis: a kind of do-it-yourself therapy in which the deep and powerful emotions of pity and fear portrayed on the stage produced equally powerful, and thereby cleansing, emotions in the audience. Not all audience reactions were positive: there are accounts of pregnant women miscarrying when the Furies appeared on the stage, so successfully did Greek drama plug into cultural fears and superstitions.

We have a deep human need for drama, which in its literal sense can be defined in one word: conflict. In this context a boxing match is as much theatre as a Royal Shakespeare Company production; there is a process of catharsis whereby members of the audience at such events (if the event is doing its job properly) find their pent-up emotions released.

Our need for drama often finds inappropriate expressions too; those individuals described in the last section who use hostility as a communication technique are creating conflict where it didn't previously exist; the person in the office next door who insists on marching about screaming 'I don't believe it!' every time they lose a paperclip is probably inspired by a subconscious impulse to make their life more dramatic than it currently is.

But there are many positive workplace applications for the theories and techniques of modern professional theatre; the company of actors is a workplace team; it is critical to the success of their project (production in the case of theatre) that they perform well as a team; outstanding individual contributions ultimately reflect on the team or the project as a whole; and individual differences, whether of personality, opinion or principle, may have to be subordinated for the good of the final deliverable. Professional actors communicate with each other, both in and out of role, and ultimately with their audience.

We are going to use this section to look at some particular topics related to theatre, drama and theatre company teamwork which have messages for day-to day workplace communication.

THE REHEARSAL

The period of rehearsal which actors undergo before a production may be a matter of weeks, days or months. Crudely, rehearsals can be seen as little more than practice for the real event. But in a good, creative theatrical team, the rehearsal is something more. It is a chance to fall flat on your face with no negative critical (or commercial) comeback. What many bad actors do is to make a decision on the first day of rehearsal exactly how their character is going to be played. They then repeat this portrayal in every rehearsal. They are indeed getting practice in performing their part; the danger is that they are also making it stale and unexciting. By the time of performance the portrayal may be one-dimensional and, effectively, over-rehearsed.

What many good actors do is to use the rehearsal period as a chance to explore all the possibilities for their character. This may involve simple variations of accent and posture; of more subtle nuances to do with pace and intonation. Whatever the variations of approach being explored, the object is not to be tied down by assumptions about the text, but to be as unconstrained as possible.

The danger comes when an actor who intends to use the rehearsal period for exploration purposes finds him- or herself in a company of actors who intend to decide what to do on day one and stick to it; in such an environment our exploratory actor will appear unacceptably maverick and disruptive, because the experimental approach requires an openness on the part of all company members: if a duologue is taking place in which one of the actors involved wants to experiment with a new way of delivering his or her lines, the actor on the receiving end of the experimentation must be prepared to react 'realistically' – that is, reflecting back the style being used by the first actor.

One important factor which restricts many actors and prevents them from feeling they are able to work in this way is, very simply, a fear of failure. The fragile ego of an actor may be an unfair stereotype in many cases, but they are, after all, only human – and all humans have an innate fear of 'showing myself up'. It may only be in front of your peers, but it is a real fear nevertheless.

So a great many actors will play it safe: make a character choice which seems reliable and stick to it, for fear any experimental departure should appear risible to the other company members. The fear of appearing incompetent is death to the creative process. Edward de Bono summed it up in a phrase we have already had cause to quote: 'The need to be right all the time is the biggest bar there is to new ideas.'

This is not the way in which good creative teams function. They thrive in an enviroment which resists being constrained by what de Bono called 'tethering factors' – those assumptions which we all have about the 'right' way to do things. Team members are not afraid to try out new approaches to tasks and problems, because they know that their colleagues all support and contribute to the experimental process. The team creates for itself a safe 'rehearsal period' in which anything and everything can be thrown into the pot. The team can then begin to come to conclusions about the right choice to make before there is any need to share publicly the results of its work.

Not enough use is made of 'rehearsal time' in most offices. There are benefits not only in the approaches just described;

how many of us, faced with an important sales meeting, will ask a colleague to role play the potential client so that we can try out as many different approaches as possible in a safe support-ive environment? We would probably resist such a rehearsal, for fear of doing something which made us appear less than com-petent in front of a colleague – as if appearing less than compe-tent in front of a potential client were the better option.

IMPROVISATION

At the opposite end of the theatrical spectrum from the rehearsed, polished theatrical production is the improvised the-atrical piece: something of a theatrical cult at the time of writing following the success of TV series such as *Whose Line Is It Any-way?* Audiences never cease to be impressed by the capacity of these performers to pluck ideas from the ether, animate them, and make them entertaining instantaneously.

Ask most actors and they will let you into a secret: improvisa-tion is not particularly difficult – at least not compared with other types of theatrical performance. Like the juggler, the improviser is at an advantage because most of his or her audi-ence have never tried to do themselves what he or she does, whereas many thousands of us belong to amateur dramatic companies and therefore feel we speak with some *gravitas* on the subject of rehearsed theatre.

What makes a good improviser is not dissimilar to the quality that makes a good 'rehearser': a resistance to the fear of failure. It's a bit like standing at the edge of a cold swimming pool: you could hover for ages wondering whether to plunge in, but once you do (especially if you leap straight in without dipping your toes in first) you're at least 90 per cent of the way there. The art of improvisation is the art of Going For It: of removing the pause before leaping in. The secret of this is that old chestnut: practice. The more one practises improvisation, the easier it gets – but it still never gets predictable, because there is never an opportunity to rehearse the substance. It is the raw creativity of improvised theatre which audiences find so entertaining and impressive.

It is probably not too outrageous a generalization to say that there is not enough improvisation in the average office. There are two concrete benefits to using improvisation techniques which make it worth consideration by managers:

- *The ability to improvise improves with practice*   We all find ourselves in situations which call upon improvisation skills: an awkward question from a superior; being caught out under-prepared during a presentation; having to brief subordinates at short notice. What most organizations do not do is encourage improvisation sessions at which the ability to plunge in can be developed. As with the rehearsal example above, it may be that a formalized arrangement encourages more participation.

- *Improvised performances are often more creative*   There are some managers who thrive on going to every meeting completely unprepared, and perhaps one or two management developers who run whole training courses without knowing in advance what they are going to do. For most individuals, however, the truth of this principle comes out more when linked to the rehearsal analogy: you will often discover more creative ways of doing things if you plunge in and try them out without preparation in a safe environment. Try out a presentation in front of a colleague before you've really prepared it finally; write a report as a first draft without worrying too much about grammatical constructions. Then go back and look at anything coming out of the exercise which can add value to the final 'true' performance.

ROLE PLAYING AND THE PLAYING OF ROLES

The most common contribution drama makes to management development is in the use of role play techniques, where an employee will practise going through a certain scenario which is relevant to his or her current and/or future work. Particular types of work for which role play is a popular training tool include debt counselling practice for bank and building society workers; dealing with difficult customers for retail or service staff; and coaching and counselling employees for people managers.

Role playing is an invaluable discipline which works on at least two levels. First of all there is what one can think of as the 'inoculation effect'. When we are inoculated against a virus, a small, safe quantity of that virus is introduced into the body. If the full-blown version ever strikes, the body can recognize it and deal with it effectively. So it is with role playing. It is an opportunity to be exposed to a small quantity of real life in the 'safe' enviroment of the peer group. If the real situation strikes, the indiviual recognizes its basic dynamics and has the where-withal to deal with it more effectively.

The other main benefit of role playing is the 'exercise effect'. Muscles left unexercised atrophy and lose their power and flexibility. Called into service unexpectedly, they are painful to use and give a substandard service. A manager who may occasionally have to deal with a difficult situation such as a disciplinary interview will benefit from regular or semi-regular role playing of that kind of interview, to ensure that his or her ability to deal with it spontaneously is adequately developed.

This is the positive side of role play. It works when it is acknowledged as artificial and used for the purposes of rehearsal. However, we also see in the workplace many examples of people whose playing of roles intrudes, and occasionally overshadows, their daily lives. This may be comparatively harmless, such as the person who enjoys playing the role of 'the busy executive' and loves to hear the sound of his or her own voice saying 'Can't talk now – I'm in a meeting' down the telephone. For many individuals, however, playing a role can lead to a denial of their true selves, or at least a reluctance to accept their own limitations.

There are various ways in which one can detect an individual who is uncomfortable playing a particular role, all derived from the theatre. One way is to look out for the 'shadow move'. Not to be confused with the 'shadow dynamic' discussed earlier, shadow moves are those gestures made by an actor which are the actor's own, rather than those of the character he or she is playing. When watching a play (especially a bad production of one), you may see the occasional actor whose eyes dart sideways to the audience now and again, or whose hands and fingers seem to twitch without focus as he or she speaks a line. Such moves display a lack of total comfort within the role: the actor is not fully 'immersed', as it were.

This type of gestural incongruity pops up in the workplace too: we see it when managers attempting to deal assertively with subordinates display body language which screams 'I don't want to be here', or when 'professional' presenters' hands twitch by their sides like restless spiders.

A vocal, rather than physical, giveaway of insecurity lies in a phonetic characteristic known as the 'strong form'. In normal phonetics, our speech is littered with what are called 'neutral' vowels. In the International Phonetic Alphabet these are denoted by the symbol ə. A neutral vowel is one which remains unstressed when the word is spoken and so is heard as a neutral sound rather than pronounced as a vowel sound. In the word 'doctor', for example, the end of the word is pronounced as a neutral vowel, rather than as the sound 'or'.

When actors attempt to use a dialect or intonation which is not their own, they run the risk of overstressing every syllable of their speech. Rather than use neutral vowels, everything emerges as 'strong forms' – you might hear them say 'doc-tor' rather than 'doctə'. The effect on the audience is to draw attention to the artifice of the chosen accent, rather than to the character using it. As with shadow moves, what we see (or in this case hear) is an actor not completely in role.

Away from the theatre, we hear strong forms used most often by individuals attempting to give themselves a veneer of authority. Received wisdom (and very misguided wisdom it is too) tells us that status is conferred by the number of long words you can pepper your speech with. Thus people trying to raise their status will use words which do not necessarily form part of their own natural vocabulary. In an attempt to display these words to full advantage, they will overstress them. Thus people unused to the media finding themselves interviewed on a TV news bulletin spray strong forms at the viewer with reckless abandon.

If you find yourself dealing face-to-face with someone displaying either of the above qualities, what should you do? Obviously, saying, 'Goodness, was that a shadow move I saw you displaying just then?' is out. Often, though, it is worth remembering that the people most likely to display these giveaways are those attempting to dominate a situation: and if you are at risk of giving in to someone because of their apparent status, then check for these signs – their status may be more flimsy than you – or they – realize.

The remedy for these afflictions is somewhat homeopathic in that treating like with like is potentially the most productive solution. Someone who is fulfilling a role that they are obviously uncomfortable with is an ideal candidate for some formalized, structured role-play work, because they can use the safe enviroment which role play provides to work through some of their anxieties about interpersonal communication. Managers responsible for 'empowering' individuals – which as far as we are concerned means providing them with a framework within which their responsibilities and freedom are increased – may want to consider this approach as an additional coaching option (see the next chapter for more on coaching).

ENTERTAINMENT VALUE

Finally, a short *cri de cœur*. The authors of this volume have lost count of the number of presentations and informal talks we have sat through which have been mind-numbingly boring – not in content, but in form. Two thoughts spring to mind:

- Sir Philip Sidney, one of the earliest literary critics, wrote in *A Defense of Poesy* that literature presents us with philosophy in the same way that a child is given medicine disguised in his or her favourite food. In other words, an audience will digest a serious message far more readily if it is presented in a palatable form. But the fear of failure, of appearing inadequate, which has dogged the 'how not to' examples which litter this section, rears its head again here. Because it is that same fear which prevents most people involved in the imparting of information from doing anything other than trying to appear as highbrow and serious as possible. This is not necessary. Take it from us. Please.

- William Shakespeare recognized that audiences watching his tragedies would not be able to sit through an entire play without needing to laugh. It is the same effect as that experienced by people who feel the urge to giggle at funerals: a need to release tension or built-up emotion. Shakespeare deliberately built comic scenes into his tragedies – thus the porter in *Macbeth* is strategically placed just after the murder of Duncan, to give the audience a legitimate opportunity for that release. Similarly, anyone making a presentation, for example, has to realize that the more serious the subject matter, the more the audience will appreciate a legitimate opportunity to laugh. And if you don't regard yourself as a gifted comic, go for another strand of entertainment: use visuals, music, perhaps even drama, to get your point across.

QUESTIONS

- Does your organization provide the freedom to try new approaches out in a safe environment before 'going live'?

- How much support exists within the organization for individuals wishing to rehearse or practise skills?

- How confident do you feel when called upon to improvise? If the answer is 'not very', what do you fear: failure? ridicule? having a lack of confidence exposed?

- How often do you play roles at work? (And how many of those around you do as well?)

TRAINING AND DEVELOPMENT GUIDELINES

Theatrical techniques and drama have been a trademark of charismatic trainers since the profession was invented; but even those who eschew this form of training have much to gain from 'acting it up'. Trainers and participants would benefit from using the training area as a rehearsal room, to experiment, to try new approaches with clear and direct feedback in a safe environment. The concept of rehearsal as a means of continuously improving one's own performance can also benefit the training activity.

The ability to improvise, or think on your feet, is a key skill for trainers as well as managers, salespeople and most others in the work environment. It means having enough confidence in your ability to react swiftly to the unexpected and not be frozen into inactivity through fear of failure.

In this section a lot has been said about roles and role playing as a common feature of training and development programmes. By specifically studying acting techniques these role-playing exercises can be developed into even better forms of training. Linked with this is the use of the voice and body in terms of communication. The actor learns to employ all his or her physical presence to communicate with the chosen audience, and although the techniques might not be suited to everyday working life, most of us could make better use of our voices and bodies in communication. Where better to learn than from the theatre?

Finally, one of the main lessons trainers can learn from the theatre is to do with entertainment. By making training entertaining and using all available tools to grip the audience's attention the message is transmitted more effectively. Some trainers mistake entertainment for frivolity and in consequence produce lecture-like training sessions in which everyone falls asleep. So theatre techniques provide a means of enhancing training performance and enlivening it at the same time.

TEAM FORMATION AND DEVELOPMENT

The model we are using in this section was developed by Will Schutz, an American psychologist who spent some time observing the behaviour of submarine crews. If we are looking at teams performing under pressure, it has to be said that a submarine crew must be something of a paradigm – cooped up together in a confined space for months on end, they must still perform their designated tasks to perfection at a moment's notice.

Schutz saw that the primary consideration for selecting the members of such a team would be the compatibility of the individuals who would be living in each other's pockets. He developed a questionnaire – now used in organizations as the FIRO-B (Fundamental Interpersonal Relations Orientation–Behaviour) – which was designed to itemize the ways in which an individual behaves towards other people. He based the questionnaire on his own model of interpersonal behaviour, which looks at what happens when a group of people get together.

THE FORMATION OF A TEAM

Schutz saw three distinct interpersonal dimensions, representing three distinct stages in group (team in this case) formation. The first dimension he called *inclusion*. The first decision any new group of individuals has to make is who's in and who's out: in other words, does the team regard all its members as equally significant and worthy of inclusion? Does everyone have a role?

We see inclusion at work in many forms. The traditional shopfloor practice of sending a colleague 'to Coventry' (ie not speaking to them, behaving as if they are not there) is effectively the group saying 'You are no longer included in our group'. When we are at school we want to be part of somebody's gang;

teenagers find fashion a vital badge of inclusion; adults can never resist cultivating devices such as the 'in joke' – only funny to those who are in the know (in other words, those who are included in that particular group).

In team terms, the inclusion questions are:

- 'Do we want to include this person in our team activities?'

- 'Do I want to be part of this particular team?'

Imposed inclusion is unsatisfactory: the members of a work team may have been picked by a senior member of staff, but the team won't really work unless all the members feel included and are happy to include each other in the team activities.

Once membership is clarified, the second dimension, that of *control*, comes into play. This is the second big decision the team makes: who's top dog? Again, an imposed leader may or may not be the right one. Teams usually decide for themselves whether they respect the leader's competence and are therefore happy to be under his or her control. The leader, too, may be uncomfortable in a controlling position and may prefer to have someone else take responsibility.

In any group of children, a hierarchy is not difficult to spot. Nobody imposes it; the children don't necessarily discuss it. Like animals, they know from relating to each other as individuals who has natural status. In a workplace team, people may be more informed about which individuals are theoretically competent to lead; but respect and trust for another person's competence can be fickle, and based on factors other than a good CV.

In each team, the control questions are:

- 'Who do we want to be in charge of us?'

- 'Do I want to control these people/be controlled by this person?'

The third dimension, and arguably the crucial one for high-performance teams, comes into play last of all. Schutz called this *openness*. This is about how close and personal we want the relationships within the group to be: how much we want to share with others, and how much we want others to share with us.

Being open with another individual is taken as a sign of their likeability – because I like you, I want to share things with you.

It goes much deeper than inclusion, which is a social dynamic (you can be included in a group without knowing any personal information about the other group members). Teams in which there is a high level of openness tend to have a positive and productive climate, because any problems which arrive are dealt with openly rather than being swept under the carpet.

Openness questions for team members are:

- 'How much do we like and trust each other?'

- 'How close and personal do we want our relationships to be?'

POLICING THE TEAM

Once the team has formed itself, any of the above three dimensions may be used to regulate the team's performance and deal with problems. Their efficacy, of course, may vary.

Teams using an inclusion strategy for self-regulation are policing themselves on the basis of 'in or out': this does not necessarily mean expulsion: you can be part of a team and still not be included in its activities. Given that inclusion is driven by awareness of others' significance, the member being excluded may simply suffer a loss of significance: their opinions are not considered worthy of attention; they are frozen out of discussions.

The opposite may happen: a disgruntled team member who disagrees with the direction the team is taking may decide to 'opt out' of the team activities. He or she remains on the team, a thorn in the side of the others as he/she abdicates from every potential consensus.

More common is the situation where the team splits into distinct factions, whose members regard each other as significant and effectively throw an inclusion cordon around themselves. The team will now fall apart, whether this is apparent to those outside it or not.

The favoured British method of policing a group is the control strategy. In this method, any member of the group who feels things have got out of hand (ie who doubts the competence of the other members) will take control 'for the good of the team' to sort things out. Success will depend on the other members' respect for the controller's competence, and whether or not they resent being controlled.

Such a strategy will run into problems if more than one member of the group decides to control things for the good of the others. Two people with no respect for each other's competence, each trying to persuade the rest of the team that he or she is the most competent for the task, can make a team meeting unproductive. Also, any member of the team for whom control is simply not an issue – that is, they neither want to control others nor be controlled themselves – will resist anyone trying to use this particular strategy.

The method of policing used most rarely, but which ultimately stands the most chance of success, is the openness strategy. The team members pursue a policy of sharing any issues, problems or fears as they arise so that they can be dealt with before they become disruptive. This is a potentially problematic approach, mainly because there will always be members of a team who, as individuals, are threatened by, or simply do not like, the idea of working with others in a close and personal way: they feel exposed when discussing feelings or private thoughts.

It is therefore important for the team to draw a distinction between what is the private property of an individual and what belongs to the team. If two members appear to be battling each other for control, the other members must be open about the fact that this may cause problems: the two individuals are not obliged to talk about the experiences they had as children which have led them to want to control others; they *are* obliged to discuss the disruption to the team's functioning that their behaviour is causing.

Many people are frightened of the openness strategy because, by definition, no one person is in control: it all seems potentially anarchic for all members to have equal rights and input. In fact, when this strategy works, the team emerges not as leaderless, but as what consultants are fond of describing as 'leader*ful*': control is automatic, because the activities of the team are controlled by their shared openness.

IMPLICATIONS

In the same way that many children display an irritating tendency to turn out like their parents, so teams very often reflect the nature of their parent organization. Organizations which place a great emphasis on inclusion – everyone must work in teams, everyone must join the social club, lots of out-of-work activities available – often produce teams where the question of who's in and who's out dominates the proceedings to an unhealthy degree. Similarly, organizations which love control – expressed in rigid hierarchies, authorization procedures and staff handbooks – look to their teams to keep everyone and everything on a tight rein and to shoehorn their activities into rigid schedules. This will tend to produce a needless sense of urgency which will inspire the control freaks to jump up and down exhorting everyone to 'just do it'.

More and more companies are struggling with the idea of openness, as the deconstruction of traditional pyramid hierarchies brings a need for closer and more trusting working relationships. Those organizations which master their intended openness cultures will be far likelier to produce teams in which members are free to deal with issues as they arise. Teams working in organizations which are still some way from this vision have to accept that, without a supportive culture, they may struggle to master an openness strategy. But, if they have read the 'natural selection' argument in Chapter 2, they can always regard themselves as mutants working for the evolution of the firm!

QUESTIONS

- How many teams (however loosely you use the term) are you currently a member of?

- Do you really want to be part of all of them?

- Do you feel part of all of them?

- Would you choose to spend time with the other team members if you were not in the same team?

- How often do you wish you could take over control of a team to 'sort everyone out'? (In other words, how competent do you regard the other members as being?)

- Do you always leave it to others to make decisions within the team?

- Do you regard the other team members as competent?

- How open and honest are you in team meetings about what you want and what you feel?

- Do you actively like the other team members? (And does it affect the way you behave in meetings?)

- What happens in your team(s) when things aren't going well? (Who takes control? Who gets frozen out? Who clams up?)

TRAINING AND DEVELOPMENT GUIDELINES

Team development is one of the most rewarding and fascinating areas of training. The reward comes from seeing groups of disparate individuals fusing together to deliver outstanding performance; the fascination comes for the trainer because team development requires team members to use a wide variety of skills – both interpersonal and problem-solving. Part of the interest also lies in the unpredictability of group dynamics. Teambuilding still has many elements of the unexpected and trainers require the ability to react and direct the team in different ways according to the stages that they are at. The Will Schutz model gives some scaffolding to this process. The dimensions of inclusion, control and openness enable the trainer to plan interventions accordingly. This framework also serves as a reminder that individuals within a team have different personal needs which often need discussion and negotiation with others if they are to be met.

For each of the dimensions there are a variety of specific exercises which the trainer can use to get people to become aware of their needs and what is happening in the team. Inclusion exercises involve selection of groups. This may seem a relatively simple task but it often generates raw emotion as participants relive the time when they were excluded from a sports team at the age of eight, or not invited to a party at thirteen. The methods that people use to avoid any possibility of being excluded are areas in which feedback can be given – very carefully of course! Control dimensions can be demonstrated with such devices as dominance lines (form a line facing the wall with the most dominant nearest the wall and the least dominant at the back – without talking). Team members can move themselves, and others, if they think they are in the wrong place. Again, what seems to be a simple exercise often produces much heat (and learning).

The final dimension – openness – is one that trainers should perhaps be cautious of unless they are skilled counsellors. Getting people to open up is fine, but only if they – and the trainer – can handle whatever comes out as a result. However, it is certainly useful to discuss what sort of interpersonal relations people are happiest with, especially within the context of a team. Some will be happy sharing their feelings and deepest thoughts, others will want communication to be fairly impersonal and task oriented.

The training implications of the model are clear: it provides the means to approach with a clear focus that complicated affair which is teambuilding. It is also a framework that can be equally well applied in areas such as organizational culture. How inclusive is the organization? How is control managed? How open are people with each other? From these questions come the rules and standards that go to make up organizational culture and the guidelines for employees' interactions with each other. And anything that is concerned with people interacting has potential for improvement through training and development.

FURTHER READING

One of the best and most readable books available on the subject of aggressive and submissive behaviour is Berne, E (1985) *Games People Play*, Ballantine, which also deals with the concept of 'I'm OK–You're OK' in more detail. Another Eric Berne book, *What do You do After You Say Hello?*, Bantam (1984), has more valuable material on interpersonal dynamics which can be readily applied to the workplace.

The Kogan Page One-Day Workshop Package Series has a set of training materials on presentations (Lowe, P (1992) *Presentation Skills*, Kogan Page/Harbridge Consulting Group) which applies theatrical techniques for the voice and the body to the art of effective presentations. For a more theatre-specific insight into creative use of the rehearsal process, try RSC actor Anthony Sher's diary account of his preparation for his critically acclaimed performance of Richard III in Sher, A (1992) *Year of the King: An Actor's Diary and Sketchbook*, Limelight Editions. Some stimulating ideas on improvisation techniques can be found in Johnstone, K (1981) *Impro*, Eyre Methuen. For anyone interested in creative use of the voice, we would also recommend, by RSC voice coach Cicely Berry (1975), *Your Voice and How to Use it Successfully*, Harrap. And if you want more on medicine disguised in children's food and how it relates to literature, Sir Philip Sidney's pearls can be found in Van Dorsten, J (ed) (1966) *A Defence of Poetry*, Oxford University Press.

As we mentioned, Will Schutz's theories are embodied in the FIRO questionnaires which are published in the UK by Oxford

Psychologists Press. The tests must be administered by a qualified practitioner, but OPP can give further help on this. Otherwise, Schutz, W (1984) *The Truth Option: A Practical Technology for Human Affairs*, Ten Speed Press, is a highly practical exploration of the theory covered in the last section of the chapter.

CHAPTER 5

Coaching and Counselling

5 COACHING AND COUNSELLING

INTRODUCTION

The ascendance of coaching as a means of developing employees is due partly to the image of the modern organization as a flatter, more flexible entity than its predecessors. In many companies today, the phrase 'direct report' has little meaning: people work in teams rather than linear reporting structures, and often within a matrix management structure which means one person may work for more than one notional boss, depending on which particular task or aspect of the organizational workload he or she is engaged in.

This structural change has begun to put an end to the 'Don't do as I do, do as I say' style of management which many of us grew up with. The need to drive responsibility and decision-making further down the organization means that the transfer of skills to employees at lower levels is vital: this process of empowerment, while terrifying to managers of the old school who see it as a threat, is a boon to many managers who are happy to delegate tasks which there is no need for them to do, to others who can acquire the skills necessary to perform those tasks.

Another strand in the story of the rise and rise of coaching is the demographic changes of recent years, with a shrinking number of school leavers and an ageing workforce. As young blood within organizations becomes at a premium, the need for flexibility and multiskilling within the workforce becomes paramount. It is for this reason (or perhaps because we now live in the 'caring nineties'!) that the welfare and development of employees has become so important. The idea of a coherent performance management process, where employees have much more involvement in their goal-setting, development and appraisal than under the old 'management by objectives' systems', has at its heart the need for individuals to be coached directly by their managers or other suitable individuals to develop both themselves and their organizational potential.

How do we define coaching? One school of thought places it on a continuum between instructing and mentoring. The former is concerned simply with defining the basics of a task and a list of 'how to's for its completion. The latter involves an interest in the employee's life development – a true mentor will work from the context of the individual's overall career path and out-of-work interests as well as his or her current job. Coaching, positioned between the two, is primarily about developing the skills necessary to grow in the job. It places far more onus on the employee than does instructing: the first stage in good coaching is to encourage the individual to develop his or her own approach to the task in question, before attempting to help him or her yourself.

Essentially, then, coaching requires that we understand individuals and their relationship to their jobs; and, more importantly, that we foster a relationship with them in which mutual respect and trust is allowed to develop. For this reason we can view the process of coaching as having a significant overlap with counselling. The joint problem-solving process which coaching requires ('Why do you think that job didn't go according to plan?') owes a lot to the process of counselling in which the 'client' is encouraged to develop an understanding of his or her own situation rather than rely on the 'agony aunt' approach (where he or she is provided with a textbook solution which may or may not work for that particular individual).

The lesson we learn from counselling is that each individual needs to be understood in terms of his or her individual motivation and way of construing the world: for the coaching process to succeed the manager must find some way of drawing broad conclusions about where an employee is 'coming from'. Some of the material in Chapter 2 is relevant to this (especially the Jungian model and the transition curve) for those managers concerned with career counselling or providing coaching within the context of career development. In this chapter we look at some models of personal development and of approaching a 'client' whose needs and motivations we may not be too familiar with.

DEVELOPING THE INDIVIDUAL

There are numerous theories relating to the human condition which rest on the concept of two complementary or opposite forces. Carl Jung, for example, defined extroversion and intro-version as two types of vital energy, the former directed towards the outer world of people and things, the latter towards the inner world of concepts and ideas.

Chinese philosophy also identifies two forms of vital energy. In definition they have some similarity with Jung's theory, but have qualities which go beyond Jung's model. The Chinese called their two types of energy yin and yang. Yin is the energy of 'relatedness': it is concerned with nourishing, connecting, and accepting others without judgement or criticism. Yang is the energy of 'separatedness'. It is concerned with establishing structure, clarity, boundaries and differences.

According to this particular philosophy, we all need both forms of energy to build and maintain our identity and relations with the world around us. Some situations will call for more of one form of energy than the other: bringing up children requires more yin, working on an analytical report requires more yang. The combination of the two energies prevalent in each individual is seen as partly inherited and partly influenced by the kinds of energy supplied to us by our parents. The Chinese view of development given below may seem unacceptably stereotypical in these enlightened times, but taken with a pinch of 1990s salt it contains a strong element of truth.

Before birth and in the child's first few years, he or she is connected to and supported by his or her mother, existing as part of her – literally before birth, then in terms of dependence. It is during these first years that the capacity for relating and trusting is developed. From the age of about five the child has to learn to act independently – in other words to separate from the mother. This is the stage at which children are seen as building boundaries between themselves and the world around them: a sense of identity begins to develop. This may happen through relating to transitional objects such as dolls; the traditional philosophy sees the father as supplying the critical energy of separatedness.

Later in the young person's development we see the energies working in powerful ways: the teenage years are a time for many young people in which separatedness becomes vital at home, but the need for individual identity is in conflict with the equally strong need to relate; peer groups become vital for supplying yin energy to compensate for the preponderance of yang at home.

With maturity we (hopefully) bring the two energies into balance: we relate to the world while maintaining our awareness of our separatedness from it. In our working lives this complementary balance is crucial: everyone within an organization needs to be able to relate and communicate with others while at the same time preserving a clarity about their own unique roles and identities. Modern management models may enshrine it in terms of the distinction between subjective and objective approaches, or between people and task issues.

THE CONSEQUENCES OF IMBALANCE

It is obviously desirable that our adult selves maintain a harmonious balance between yin and yang energy; but, as we are all painfully aware, achieving harmonious ideals in life is a prerequisite more honoured in the breach than the observance. A preponderance of one type of energy over the other leads to an imbalance with tangible effects on interpersonal behaviour.

* *Lack of ability to relate*   A lack of yin energy may result from an over-authoritarian upbringing (and therefore an overemphasis on yang energy) or an excessive emphasis on achievement in formative years. The result in adulthood is that the individual finds it difficult to build relationships with other people that are relaxed and trusting. He or she may easily feel rejected and anxious. The internal effects may be a lack of feeling of warmth, a lack of acceptance of oneself. An individual with this kind of imbalance will be driven (as our notional teenager was in the example above) to look for the missing yin energy he or she was denied in childhood, often by forming relationships in which he or she is submissive, playing a child role to the other individual's parent.

In many cases, the lack of yin energy is compensated for by an overdeveloped yang: in this case the individual is able to create a 'mask' to hide behind (see Figure 5). He or she will build impersonal relationships in which the focus is on shared task-oriented concerns (such as a relationship which focuses on a shared hobby, or an evening's drinking with people from the same department at work). He or she may try to control relationships in order to keep an imposed structure on them and therefore to keep at arm's length any threat of intimacy and true 'relatedness'.

Too much yang: emphasis on doing/
the objective; over-focused

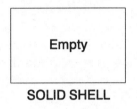

SOLID SHELL

Too much yin: emphasis on being/
the subjective; over-diffuse

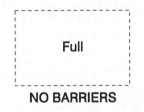

NO BARRIERS

Figure 5 *Consequences of energy imbalance*

- *Lack of ability to discriminate* An underdeveloped yang can arise from a lack of emphasis on individual responsibility during formative years (the stereotypical cause is the over-possessive mother). It leads in adulthood to an individual who finds it difficult to act independently, to initiate action. Such people may find it difficult to structure their lives, and will look for others to do this for them. In a work environment, they are often those who persistently 'pass the buck' or find ways to avoid accepting accountability when things go wrong. Individuals with underdeveloped Yang may have a problem with authority figures, tending either to idolize them or reject them, without being able to take an objective view.

Historically, as can be seen from some of the assumptions that the original philosophy makes, yin energy has been seen as being essentially feminine and yang as masculine. Given that the ideal is a balance between both energies regardless of whether you are a man or a woman, there are, however, some distinct effects of imbalance between the sexes which go some way to underpinning the nature of the roles men and women are expected to fill in life.

A woman with an underdeveloped yin will not be able to conform to society's expectations of her as supportive, caring and nurturing at her own expense. Women who appear to deny this side of their characters in pursuit of task-oriented career goals may simply be displaying an overemphasized yang. Similarly, men with a lack of yang energy may have trouble living up to the male image of a tough-minded, task-focused decision maker, and may suffer in environments where this is required. They may also deny this side of their personalities, and reject in excessive ways the masculine values which their lack of yang denies them.

Male and female stereotypes are challenged head on, and often aggressively by the two examples above; but are reinforced by the other two possibilities for imbalance. A woman with a lack of yang energy will overplay the stereotype of the helpless female; a man with a lack of yin energy will behave as an unfeeling, macho machine. All four examples are equally damaging both to the cause of equal opportunities and to the potential for individuals to develop themselves as 'whole' human beings.

IMPLICATIONS FOR COACHING

In order to be successful, the coaching process requires both yin and yang energy. Successful coaching relies on an open, trusting relationship between manager and subordinate: the manager is 'nourishing' the subordinate in a role which is in a sense parental; judgement and criticism often need to be suspended on both sides in the early stages of the process.

If this 'yin' approach is the bedrock which allows the coaching relationship to flourish, successful output depends on adequate yang input. The subordinate needs to be guided towards a state of clarity about the identity of the task in question, where the job responsibilities begin and end, and what the subordinate's exact role is in the new process of which he or she is a part. The empowerment which lies at the heart of coaching also requires that the subordinate be capable ultimately of making decisions in the new area in which he or she has been coached.

It can be useful, too, for those with responsibility for coaching others to think of individuals in terms of which of the two forms of energy they appear to display most. An individual who is under-yanged and over-yinned, revealed in a lack of ability to discriminate, will need a coaching method which utilizes his or her preferred energy (and therefore concentrates on the relationship, with the manager providing structure and decisiveness), but which ultimately needs to emphasize yang-type skills: the subordinate needs to be encouraged to develop in the areas of decision-making, creating structure and clarity, etc, in order to be able to approach tasks in a fully adaptable way.

Similarly, a subordinate who appears to be over-yanged and/or under-yinned, revealed in a lack of ability to relate, will need to be held at arm's length initially and treated in a task-focused way. Trust in the relationship will develop if the manager does not breach the invisible barrier which this individual may have set up. Ultimately, however, the coaching relationship needs to be developed to encourage the subordinate to accept a more open, personal way of working without judgement or suspicion about the motives involved.

QUESTIONS

* Do your coaching methods make full use of yin and yang styles? (Do you invest as much energy – literally – in building a nurturing, trusting relationship as in providing structure and task focus?)

* Do you find that different individuals respond differently to the two broad styles? (And can you relate this to any broad conclusions about their own balance?)

- How clear are you about the dominant 'energies' of those you are responsible for? About your own?

(**Note:** As much of the coaching process is a form of training in itself, we have not included specific training and development guidelines in each section: an overview will be found at the end of the chapter.)

FACILITATING SELF-IMPROVEMENT

In the nineteenth century, a working actor named F Mathias Alexander became intrigued by the regularity with which he lost his voice during theatrical performances. He wondered whether it could be related to the stress of performance, and its effect upon his body. As a result of diligent self-observation, he discovered that when he was on stage, he tended to tilt his head back at a far more extreme angle than he would use in everyday life. The result was a greater strain on his larynx, and ultimately a regular loss of voice.

The Alexander technique (or principle, depending on whom you hear about it from) grew out of this simple yet powerful discovery: there is a distinct relationship between body posture and our overall efficiency, whether stress-related or not. Central to the principle of correct alignment is the 'head–neck' relationship, as F Mathias discovered to his cost. Seasoned Alexander enthusiasts place the alignment of the head on the neck as crucial to control of the body's relaxation: a badly positioned head can lead to rising shoulders, which places tension on the torso, affects the way we walk and sets up cycles of tension throughout the body.

Studying the alignment of the body in depth in this way reveals a number of flaws in traditional assumptions about posture. For a start, the old 'shoulders back, stomach in, chest out' doctrine has no place among Alexander practitioners, who will point to an 'ideal' (or economic) posture as being constructed around:

- A head positioning which places the crown of the head at the highest point in the body (which means holding the chin lower than most people would choose to).

- Shoulders held naturally low and forward (as opposed to back and up around the ears).

- The pelvis sitting in a forward position (so that the buttocks are effectively 'tucked under' the body).

- The knees relaxed and very slightly bent.

If this description conjures up bizarre pictures in the mind of the reader, it must be emphasized that the central principle of this technique is *not* to try and do the 'right thing': to force the body into the posture described above is as potentially stressful as to force it into a 'stomach in, chest out' posture. The aim is to try *not to do the wrong thing*: that is, rather than force yourself into the ideal posture, develop an awareness of your body that enables you to monitor when you are slipping into a bad posture, and trying to inhibit that negative, rather than accentuate the positive.

The ability of an individual to control his or her body in this way is obviously questionable, since if one has reached such a height of self-awareness, stress may not be a particularly central problem. But it is possible, with practice, to develop a way of thinking which allows muscles to relax under instruction from the brain: it is not so far away from the way that our brain instructs the muscles in the arm to pick something up, or commands the leg muscles to walk. In many ways it is a discipline not unrelated to the Zen approach we looked at in Chapter 3 – encouraging a space in your mind in which you can be aware of how your body is being misdirected.

One key concept which is relevant here is that of 'inhibition'. This is used by followers of the technique not in its accepted sense of social shyness, but in the way that we used it above, in terms of inhibiting the learned muscular reactions which set up stressful responses. It is another version of the old adage 'count to ten before you lose your temper'. Basically, the principle is that if we allow ourselves to react immediately to stressful stimuli, our muscles respond by tensing ready for whatever action may be required. By pausing before reacting, we wait a moment until the 'urgency' has passed, and then respond in a more conscious, deliberate way.

Economy of energy is at the heart of the technique. The idea is to ensure that no muscle is used in a wasteful way. To see an enlightening example of the lack of economy most of us employ in our everyday lives, watch yourself in the mirror next time you are cleaning your teeth. All that is needed to accomplish this task is to open the mouth, lift the arm and, through wrist and elbow movements, to brush the teeth with the brush. Yet most people watching themselves will notice an alarming multiplicity of muscular reactions: we lift our shoulders, move our head around instead of the arm, tense parts of our bodies which have no part to play in the task . . . the list is endless.

To summarize, the main aims of those who practise the Alexander technique are:

- to allow the body to align itself in a relaxed way;

- to inhibit stressful muscular responses;

- to find the most economical way of performing physical tasks.

IMPLICATIONS FOR COACHING

The central principle of the Alexander technique is a wonderful maxim for self-improvement: *Don't try to do the right thing, try not to do the wrong thing.* Much energy is wasted by managers attempting to fit themselves into a model of working that is not ideal for them. It is far better to work out what it is one should *not* do, and look out for that.

The role of the coach in this context is twofold: the first aspect is to assist in the process of identifying unsuitable ways of approaching tasks, and to help identify reasons why certain approaches have not worked. Manager and subordinate then need to work together to develop methods of avoiding unsuitable working practices.

The second aspect of the coaching role is to observe the subordinate on the job, in order to help him or her avoid 'trying to do the right thing'. The subordinate in this case needs an outside eye to identify points at which he or she is attempting to follow a textbook approach which may not be appropriate either for the personality and strengths of the subordinate, or for the specific nature of the job.

In both these examples the coach is playing a facilitation role, in the same way that an Alexander teacher will facilitate the alignment of an individual's body by talking him or her through relaxation techniques and by helping him or her to identify areas of misalignment. The manager in a coaching role is facilitating optimum alignment of individual and task, by talking the individual through 'how not to's and by helping the individual develop an awareness of what is and is not appropriate to the requirements of a particular task.

The other strand of the Alexander principle, that of economy of effort, has an obvious relevance to individual on-the-job development, and therefore also to the coaching process. Individuals need to be guided through new tasks in a way which encourages them to find the path of least resistance.

Economy in all things is a doctrine much talked about, but rarely practised effectively: from time management to problem solving, to holding effective meetings, to giving presentations, all of us waste energy by taking a kind of 'spray and pray' approach to tasks, or by not knowing when to stop. The concept of inhibition is useful here: the coach can play a useful role in encouraging the habit of pausing before approaching each task; the individual should aim to inhibit his or her natural impulse, which may be to steam in and worry about method later, or to do it in a way that worked for some other task he or she approached recently. A brief reflection, helped by the coach, on the method which may be most appropriate to this particular task, may well pay dividends.

The self-audit which users of the Alexander technique conduct on their bodies is a useful discipline for managers, especially those involved in on-the-job learning. When engaged in new or comparatively unfamiliar tasks, individuals should be encouraged to stop what they are doing every so often and ask themselves: 'What am I doing and is it appropriate? Is it economical?'

QUESTIONS

- To what extent does your organization require managers to 'do the right thing'? (And how clear are employees about the wrong way to do things?)

- How economical are your approaches to tasks?

- Do you look at those people you are responsible for and see examples of wasted effort but feel unable to come up with an answer?

- How often do you pause before taking on a new task and check whether the way you *impulsively* feel you want to do it is right?

COACHING AND WORKPLACE RELATIONSHIPS

In the section on communication and teamwork we looked at Will Schutz's model of behaviour – inclusion, control and openness – with its associated underlying feelings – significance, competence and likeability. These terms and their implications are also of great help to those involved in coaching others, because achieving an awareness of one's use of these dimensions, and how appropriate they are in certain situations, can be essential to increasing on-the-job effectiveness.

INCLUSION

As we saw in the last chapter, an ability to participate in group activities is no small help when it comes to the modern organization, with its emphasis on cross-functional teamworking. The trend towards 'networking' – establishing an informal chain of contacts within and outside the organization who exchange information and provide mutual assistance – also relies on the ability (if not the preference) to relate to people on a social level. Those of us who would rather shut ourselves away in a small room and get our heads down may appear to achieve more at the end of the day, but may also threaten the social fabric of the organization which, as formal hierarchies disappear with increasing rapidity, may be all that holds a company together. We read more often about organizations that have traded in their desks for groups of armchairs where managers congregate to exchange ideas and information; organizations where 'hot desking' systems mean that no one has a 'territory' of their own, where including others and being included oneself can be of vital importance.

The manager in a coaching relationship with a subordinate needs to be aware of the extent to which inclusion is an issue with this particular person. Does his or her job require a lot of 'social' contact with others? How adept is the subordinate at handling these situations? Very often individuals who are uncomfortable dealing with people face-to-face get little support from their superiors – partly because it may not appear to be directly relevant to the task in hand, partly because it is regarded as too 'personal' an issue to deal with in a coaching environment.

In fact, if handled carefully the issue need never become 'personal' – or at least it can be approached from the standpoint that 'everything is positive'. If you are dealing with a subordinate who tends not to include people in his or her activities, but who is not too worried about being included him- or herself in the activities of others, then there is no reason why that needs to be presented as a bad thing. Rather than bad, it may rather be regarded as something which may cause difficulties in relation to the job, unless the subordinate can artificially find a way of generating the behavioural skills needed. (In the same way, if an accountant hates maths, that is not a *bad* thing in itself, provided that he or she has the mathematical skills to fulfil the requirements of the job.)

What the coach must concentrate on is working with the subordinate to identify the inclusion skills necessary for the particular use he or she needs to make of them. Is it a question of being able to contribute effectively and selflessly in a team environment? Of being able to make clients and potential clients feel 'at home'? Of being able to relate on a social level to his or her own subordinates? Remember the underlying issues to do with significance which we discussed in the last chapter: in a counselling situation these may be worth discussing.

There are, of course, negative aspects to the use of inclusion: if you are dealing with an individual who persistently gets involved with the business of others, who seems unable to work alone, or who is always attempting to become involved in workplace activities which should be no concern of theirs, then some coaching in the opposite direction may be required!

CONTROL

The appropriate use of control is a contentious issue in most organizations: we can all name individuals within our own sphere who have to be 'top dog' all the time, as well as individuals who never accept responsibility for anything and always have to be told what to do. We also meet individuals whose attitude is: 'Don't tell me what to do, and I won't tell you what to do.'

All three types can be equally damaging to the smooth running of the organization: the hardest job for a manager to learn is when to take control and when to let go. The former is essential if the manager is to be truly accountable, the latter is vital if effective delegation is to take place, and subordinates are to feel respected and rewarded.

Control is often a problem in the case of newly promoted managers. You will remember from the last chapter that the underlying feeling associated with the dimension of control is *competence*. Young managers often over-exhibit a tendency to control people and situations for one of two reasons: either they are unsure of how competent their staff are, and so tend to assume that everyone is incompetent (and that they will therefore have to do everything themselves); or they feel insecure about their own competence, and feel obliged to convince everyone that they really deserve to be a manager – usually by trying to do everything at once, even those tasks in which they are genuinely incompetent.

The coach working with managers in the former situation needs to facilitiate and develop managers' understanding that their subordinates are more than capable of performing *certain* tasks: the important thing is for them to be willing to try to ascertain exactly which tasks each subordinate is competent in, so that they can be encouraged to delegate effectively. In the latter situation, the coach must work in counselling mode to help managers understand and be honest about exactly what areas they are truly competent in, which areas they *need* to be competent in, and which areas can safely be delegated to someone else.

The coach will be doing a greater service than they may realize if a manager with excessive use of control can be corrected early in his or her career. Will Schutz described individuals exhibiting high 'expressed' control (ie wanting constantly to control people and situations) and low 'wanted' control (ie never wanting to be controlled by others) as 'Mission Impossible' types: such a person is on a lifelong crusade to be competent in everything. He or she is doomed to failure, of course; but the almost paranoiac need to display competence will not allow people like this to admit failure even to themselves.

As a result, these individuals drive themselves harder and harder and either burn themselves out or continue to follow a blighted path in which they never discover true fulfilment because there is always another peak left unconquered: another stone unturned; another competency not signed off. We attempted to counsel a manager in his late forties whom the FIRO-B (Schutz's own test designed to measure these dimensions) reported as falling into the Mission Impossible category. The suggestion that it might pay him to ease off a little brought a torrent of abuse – quite an extensive torrent. Most revealing of all, however, was when the torrent came to an end, and he finished by saying: 'And the worst thing is my wife's been saying exactly the same thing to me for twenty years – and she doesn't know what the hell she's talking about either!'

What is the 'ideal' control pattern? Certainly the ability to take control is more useful to a manager than a penchant for being controlled. A ratio of occasions to take control to occasions to let go probably works out at about 3:1 – but there is obviously no blanket rule. Certainly, as far as someone in a coaching role is concerned, it is of paramount importance to persuade your subordinate to accept that everyone is incompetent in some things – it is those people who try and prove their competence in all things who will never achieve true competence – because while you're pretending to be competent, someone else with more humility is busy asking someone in a coaching role to help them plug the gaps in their knowledge and skills.

OPENNESS

If control is the dimension which causes the most difficulty, openness is the dimension which presents the biggest challenge. Yet, as far as anyone concerned with coaching subordinates is concerned, it is absolutely vital if meaningful communication within the coaching relationship is to take place. A coach who is going out of his or her way to be open with a subordinate, but who is met by a closed mind or indifference, is not going to get very far. Similarly, a coach who attempts to keep the relationship at arm's length is closing the door on a great deal of richness and potential benefit.

We are not saying that individuals who hesitate to turn every relationship into a close, personal, sharing event cannot be good coaches. We must remember that, as pointed out in the introduction to this chapter, there is a distinction to be made between the mentor – who takes a truly personal approach to developing subordinates – and the coach – who is concerned with facilitating on-the-job development. Nevertheless, as a coach you are asking the subordinate under you to expose a certain amount about him- or herself – to adopt a vulnerable position, whether because of admitting lack of competence in a particular area or because of having to accept your own interventions. For that reason, if for no other, you owe it to the subordinate to give a little of yourself in return.

The underlying feeling associated with open behaviour is likeability. The proposition is: 'I reveal something of myself to you because I like you; if you like me you will do the same.' There is a genuine dilemma attached to this rather simple equation. The most obvious aspect of this is that we may genuinely not like the person we are responsible for coaching; they may not like us. Yet if the relationship is to succeed it must in effect say: 'We trust each other enough to share a certain amount of personal information about ourselves.'

Think of it from a tactical point of view. If your subordinate can trust you, he or she is more likely first of all to accept your help and advice, and second to feel prepared to reveal something about his or her own feelings about work and job readiness. Therefore, if you as a coach can find an easy way of establishing some form of openness it will pay dividends in terms of increased performance.

Some years ago a survey was carried out to look at what made unhappily married couples unhappy. The researchers went to the wives first of all. They asked, simply, 'What is it about your husband that makes you unhappy?' Money, sex, and various other predictable answers came somewhere in the top ten, but the top two responses were 'My husband doesn't appreciate me enough,' and 'My husband doesn't express his feelings enough.' (Well, you'd expect women to say that about men wouldn't you?)

The researchers then went to the unhappily married husbands and asked them what it was about their wives that made them unhappy. Surprise, surprise, the top two answers were 'My wife doesn't appreciate me enough,' and 'My wife doesn't express her feelings enough.'

Being good scientific individuals, the researchers did a control experiment and talked to happily married couples as well. They asked wives: 'If there was something you could change about your husband, what would it be?' Top two answers: 'Well, it would be nice if my husband appreciated me a bit more, and if he expressed his feelings a bit more.' And when they asked the husbands they got the same response.

All of us, in the UK at least, seem to be walking around with a massive appreciation deficit: our standpoint is: 'I'll show you mine if you show me yours.' Coaching relationships, and manager/subordinate relationships of all kinds, suffer from this same syndrome: we don't want to be too open in case it gets thrown back in our faces; but we would appreciate it if the other person would be a bit more open with us. As the coach, it's up to you to make the first move: the results may surprise you!

QUESTIONS

- What is the appropriate level of inclusion behaviour for your organization?

- Do managers know when to take control and when to let go?

- Do you?

- Do you like the people you are responsible for? Your own manager?

- How much appreciation do you want for the way you do your job? Do you get it?

TRAINING AND DEVELOPMENT GUIDELINES

This chapter has concentrated on the coaching aspect of the developmental spectrum rather than 'pure' training. But it is a fact that trainers have to be good coaches if they are to be successful in conveying skills and knowledge. There are very few people in this world who can immediately put things they have learned into practice without trying them out first. Practice is only effective if there is coaching feedback and support and hence the good trainer will also want to play the coach wherever possible and see the process of competency development through to a successful conclusion. If trainer and coach are different people (it may be the line manager who is ultimately accountable for on-the-job development of individuals) then the organization must have a training and development policy which ensures that everyone is clear what the development objectives are, and where training and coaching fit into the overall goals for each individual. Managers must feel able to approach training staff about the best way to tackle particular issues, and trainers should always refer to line managers for information about the strengths, weaknesses and preferences of particular individuals.

The first section of this chapter emphasized the need for balance in everyone between relating skills (yin) and skills of discrimination and objective analytical thought (yang). As has been mentioned in other training guidelines sections of this book, it is vital that the trainer and/or coach is aware of his or her own balance and make-up and the effect that this has on personal performance. Clarity on this point will make it easier and more effective to apply the ideas to the development of others. People with lots of yin will need and want lots of support and may be overly sensitive to criticism and feedback; people with an orientation towards yang will want clear-cut facts and ideas without any woolly orientation towards feelings and subjectivity. Yet the trainer, if he or she is to help individuals develop, must also help the yin-dominant individual to become more discriminatory and the yang-dominant person to relax and enjoy the process of human contact. No small task!

The principle trainers can draw on from the Alexander technique is to see themselves as there not to show participants the right thing to do, but to help them not to do the wrong thing; in other words, to get rid of the blocks and barriers that impede their progress. Finally, the Schutz model gives a clear framework for trainers to evaluate their own styles of interaction with participants. Do you see yourself as working in concert with participants on a training programme, or does it feel more like 'us and them?' Are participants involved in decisions about structure, content and timetabling, or do you retain control? How personal are you in sharing experiences? Is the teaching room atmosphere formal, or relaxed and open? Can participants bring up personal concerns or is the focus strictly on task? There are no right ways of doing these things, but good trainers ensure they are true to their own needs and preferences.

The overriding message of this chapter has been the need to approach people as individual human beings with distinct needs. This may be a tall order for a trainer faced with a room containing

20 people all with different learning styles, but even bearing this principle in mind can be enough to create a more person-centred image – just as for Alexander enthusiasts it is often enough to allow your mind to think about relaxing a particular muscle.

FURTHER READING

The theories and techniques in this chapter in many ways speak for themselves – or at least are less tangential than some of our other material. As with the other chapters, we have restricted this list to books which deal directly with the theories rather than with coaching, and for this reason the list is a model of brevity.

As with Zen, it is difficult to find a book which pins down yin and yang into an easily digestible form, but a useful reference work (in English) is Gibran, K (1926), *The Prophet*, Heinemann, which deals with a number of topics related to this philosophical area.

Anyone interested in pursuing the Alexander technique is strongly advised to contact a qualified practitioner: like all beautifully simple principles, it can be disastrous in the wrong hands. For more on the theory itself and its corporeal applications, try Barker, S (1991) *Alexander Technique: Learning to Use Your Body for Total Energy*, Bantam.

Schutz, W (1984) *The Truth Option*, Ten Speed Press, is absolutely essential reading for anyone interested in the development and empowerment of individuals, and brings together the themes explored in this chapter.

CHAPTER **6**

Living With Change

6 LIVING WITH CHANGE

INTRODUCTION

Change is a constant. It may appear to us to be more frenetic or rapid than it was 10 or 20 years ago, or perhaps it is simply that faster and more global communication systems are bombarding us with information on an ever wider range of issues. Whatever the truth about the rate of change, the very fact of change and the uncertainty that it brings is a cause of not inconsiderable stress for many people. In organizations people have to adapt to new requirements, skills and structures. Managing change is now seen as one of the top managerial priorities, and the implementation of change as an area wherein skills are too often lacking. This is especially true of the effect of change on people, where any intervention is in danger of being too little, too late.

Like any vast amorphous topic, change benefits from being looked at in bite-sized chunks – or at least in mouthfuls. First, there is change that is external to individuals – such as a change of job, a change in one's own organization, or a new or changed relationship. If the change does not have an internal impact on us (in other words, we do not have to make any changes within ourselves in order for the change to happen) then we stand a better chance of being able to deal with it.

Things become more problematic when the change is internal to ourselves and we have to change our internal mental structures – the way we see the world, the classifications that we use in order to represent it. These may be objective (knowledge and skills) or subjective (our views, values, and self-image). Having to change our personal system of beliefs convinces us that, up till now, our personal vision of the world must have been incomplete or flawed in some way – which is what makes change so traumatic for some people.

A positive way of looking at this type of change is to call it 'learning' – which is, after all, a means by which we assimilate new experiences into a personal model which means something to us. But learning, of course, means admitting that we have to let go of where we were and develop something new – which people who are locked into a self-image which convinces them they are already competent find very difficult to do.

While this internal change process is going on, we will almost certainly feel confused, and possibly depressed or anxious, because we have to look at the world through different eyes. What is needed desperately at this stage is to encourage rather than resist these uncomfortable feelings. This is a period of introspection and reflection, during which old certainties must be broken down to make way for new insights.

This process is described by social anthropologists in terms of the rite of passage. Well structured and socially aware societies accept that certain changes require time and social support for them to be effective. The rite of passage from childhood to adolescence is a prime example. Many so-called 'primitive' societies have well-established rituals which, though potentially traumatic for the participants, achieve the transition from boy to man, girl to woman, in a comparatively short space of time with no after-effects. In Western society, we draw no clear line between child and adult, and in consequence adolescence drags on and on.

In keeping with this book's focus on the parallel paths of individual development and organization development, we take an individual-centred approach to dealing with change in the sections within this chapter. We start, however, with complexity theory, a new model from the world of physics which we can use to view apparently turbulent and changeful organizational environments in a comparatively simple way. The section which follows it looks at notions of 'creating', which deals with the power of the individual to produce objects, systems, relationships, or anything else in a way that is right for that individual, without succumbing to received wisdom about the correct procedure for thinking creatively.

As we move to the third section of the chapter we develop what is the principal coping style we espouse for dealing with change, the principle of choice. In other words, the way we choose to look at the world determines the way the world interacts with us. Once this principle is accepted everything becomes simultaneously more terrifying and more liberating: terrifying because the idea that we have a large degree of responsibility for what happens to us means that the world, other people, even our parents can no longer be blamed, which leaves one person to carry the can – ourselves; and liberating because all too often the habit of blaming others and external forces leads to a personal sense of loss of power, helplessness and decreased self-esteem.

An example of the need to separate the effects of change from our choice of how to deal with them can be seen in the changes in the British National Health Service. There is a great deal of anger and bitterness within the service about the move to a market-oriented style of organization, and also a great deal of enthusiasm. In looking at the changes, however, it is vital to separate the question of whether the changes are right or wrong from the fact that they are already taking place – and will go on taking place. Those individuals who will ultimately do best within the system are those who take the realistic point of view that, like it or not, the change is happening and they can choose whether to make the best of it and find a way of making it work for them, or whether to 'opt out' in protest and lose a job in the process.

We deal with this theme under the heading of 'Positive Thinking' and look at techniques used by individuals who are successful at dealing with change and uncertainty through changing the way they think.

Finally, we deal with that old devil, time, and look at how our attitudes to managing it can affect our success at dealing with changing environments. We bring together ancient Chinese thinking with more recent neuro-linguistic programming concepts to see if it is possible to develop a personal relationship with time which increases our control over change and its ravages.

COMPLEXITY MADE SIMPLE

Devotees of chaos theory will know that complex systems are, by their very nature, resistant to prediction. It is impossible, for example, to say what the weather will be like in ten days' time. The laws governing a system such as the weather may or may not be complex in themselves: they may be very simple. The unpredictability comes from the impossibility of gathering enough data in detail precise enough to allow completely accurate prediction – and from the fact that weather systems, for example, are subject to a randomness to which British umbrella wielders can testify with some passion.

Scientists have now moved beyond chaos and have come up with an elaborated version – complexity theory. Complexity has been defined as a zone lying between stability and predictability on one side, and chaos and unpredictability on the other. This is why the phrase 'the edge of chaos' is often used to describe complexity (although 'the edge of stability' would apply equally well).

In stability nothing changes. In chaos too much changes for there to be any real learning. In the complexity zone, however, systems adapt, learn and grow. Scientists have derived certain laws, and made some assumptions about complexity which can be specifically applied to organizational life.

MANAGING COMPLEXITY

The trick of managing complexity, as many organizations are discovering, lies in walking this fine line between stability and chaos. Too much change and freedom and the system will tip over into chaos – as when a company gives every manager authority to purchase without adequate cost controls. Too little innovation and the system becomes rigid, and unable to respond in any way other than its own tried and tested methods.

This is why running an organization is often seen as an art rather than a science – there needs to be constant monitoring of the system to see which way it's heading. If it is becoming too stable then change and a degree of freedom needs to be introduced to push it back – perhaps through decentralization and the creation of an entrepreneurial culture. Conversely, if there is too much change and the system is going into meltdown, restraints and disciplines need to be reinforced. Just as riding a bike, scientifically speaking, involves a constant process of correcting the front wheel alternately to left and right, so the organization needs constant readjustment between stability and chaos. The economic cycles of a country can also be seen as necessary corrections along the path to true happiness – assuming you support whichever party is in power!

RULES FOR WALKING THE TIGHTROPE

Another critical finding about complexity is that even highly complex systems can be kept on track by just a few rules governing the interaction of their constituent units – providing they are the right rules. The flight of a flock of birds, for example, looks extremely complicated, but computer models of flocks of birds in flight have shown that the whole system is based on three rules:

1. Follow the leader.

2. Move towards the centre.

3. Don't get closer than (say) three feet from another bird.

The implications of this for organizations are considerable. The spirit of this theory says that after setting a direction for the organization, the most important thing a leader can do is to focus on the 'rules' that govern interaction between people in the organization. (By 'rules' we mean not just those specifically written down, but all those informally understood and agreed to, often without any conscious acknowledgement.) Take communication processes, for example. If an organization exists in which there are no rules governing communication then the result is chaos – everyone is overwhelmed by memos, phone calls and meetings. If you go to the other extreme, where the rules might state that communication with another employee can only take place via the leaders of your respective departments, then the result is stability, with little opportunity for change through learning.

Leaders must look at these rules and adjust them where appropriate – preferably not through an internal memo but by role modelling and 'walking the talk'. This is what Jack Welch, chief executive of General Electric in the US, did when he decided that the organization had become over-bureaucratized and set out to free up the systems by giving more creative power to individual managers. He did this, however, in a formalized way which avoided the whole enterprise tipping over into chaos.

Pushing the boundaries set by over-stable rules leads to the natural selection model we discussed in Chapter 2 – natural selection being a key example of a system on the edge of chaos.

Complexity theory also tells us that it is impossible to predict what will happen to the overall shape and function of the system when rules are altered. In other words, you might change the rules governing authority for certain management actions and expect the organization to become more dynamic and flexible – but quite how it will do this is essentially unpredictable. This is why top-down change can be so dangerous and unprofitable, in terms of producing results completely different from those intended. Organizations which think that they can control the culture change process to produce tightly specified outcomes are learning that it does not work like that. Complexity theory expresses this scientifically, but philosophers like Karl Popper in his attacks on top-down planning in society have been saying something similar for many years. In addition, as we saw in Chapter 2, empirically based studies have shown that major change usually comes about because of a mutant sub-culture which spreads within the organization and takes over because it has found a better way of dealing with the world.

The implications of all this for management development professionals is profound. First, it reinforces the emphasis on individual skills and understanding – especially in terms of interpersonal interaction. Complexity theory essentially says: if you change the way that X interacts with Y within the organization, the whole organization will change, culture and all. Second, grand organizational development schemes will not work unless all the implications for potential changes in the rules of interaction are taken into account (and probably not even then). Someone is needed to provide the expertise to comment on and help to change these rules – it might as well be management developers! Finally, if training does not appear to work, the management developer has a ready-made excuse that complexity theory does not enable success to be predicted with certainty.

QUESTIONS

- Where is your organization on the stability–complexity–chaos continuum?

- How well does your organization adapt and learn?

- What measures are used to push the organization away from stability to complexity, or back from chaos to complexity?

- What are the key rules that govern interactions in your organization?

- What effect do these rules have on the organization's effectiveness?

- How is change implemented in the organization: top-down or bottom-up?

- How are environmental changes monitored and reacted to?

TRAINING AND DEVELOPMENT GUIDELINES

Some of the implications for trainers have been mentioned in the body of this section: the emphasis on individual interaction, for example, and the difference that this can make to an organization. The essential message is that everyone can make a profound difference to an organization by changing their own behaviour and the rules that they follow in dealing with other people. There are parallels here with the topics on career development and training discussed in Chapter 2.

For the trainer, the guidelines come back to the importance of convincing people of the impact that increased individual skills can have on the organization. For example, people usually find it difficult to give and receive positive, constructive feedback. If training concentrates on these two skill sets, then individual performance will be significantly affected; as individual performance improves so will that of the organization. The organization will be able to respond to its customers or its environment quickly because of the ability of people in it to receive feedback. In other words, the organization will become a learning organization, a term that is comparatively new but which is increasingly being used to describe the way that the most effective organizations develop. All this will have happened because of a simple increase in skills at an individual, interpersonal level. In other words, something which is often presented as a potentially difficult and complex topic – the learning organization – can be achieved in a relatively straightforward way.

So for the trainer there is no need to go into complex intellectual realms: just concentrating on basics and continuing to reinforce the chosen messages about essential skills will produce far-reaching and crucial business effects. In a sense, this is a back-to-basics message, but one that the trainer can use to point the way forward. It is only fair, however, to point out that complexity theory is still relatively young, and there may well be further lessons for management development arising from the theory.

CREATING OR CREATIVITY?

Everyone – but everyone – enjoys creating. There seems to be a tendency in life, however, for individuals to be labelled as 'creative' and 'non-creative', the latter group being effectively banned from creating anything. What is the difference between creating and creativity, and what are the implications for individuals and organizations?

There is a deep satisfaction in bringing something into being (or some*one*, as most parents will testify) which did not exist before. All of us are capable of creating – the criteria for judging what we create should be up to us as individuals, not to others. Frank Lloyd Wright was once asked how he knew he was a good architect. He replied, simply, 'I know.' Many would interpret this as arrogance, but he expressed something of the truth of the process of creating. If we recognize that creating is for the individual, any other benefits (such as critical acclaim) being nice but not essential, then we can be freed from the many constraints we and others place on our individual creative processes – and hopefully become more liberated and empowered as a result.

BREAKING AWAY

This process of creative liberation centres on the need to transcend the rules which we learn during childhood and which often govern large proportions of our lives. Creating has no magic formula – another problem for many individuals who feel unhappy with ambiguity, and tend therefore to steam into situations with a view to finding out what is missing and lighting up all the dark corners. Confusion is a necessary step in creating – it implies newness, and means that the essence of creating is a venture into the unknown. When we were children mistakes were not mistakes, just different ways of doing things. Unfortunately the punishments which rain down on children's heads as a result of this experimentation lead most of us as adults to believe that experimentation brings retribution – and hence that it is safer not to create. (Related to this is the idea of fear of failure which we discussed in Chapter 4.)

The beginning of creating is the process of seeing, hearing, touching *anew*. This involves leaving behind the rules which govern how we normally do things. Managers can learn a lot from some of the psychological lessons of creative arts such as drawing. Based on past experience, for example, our brain tells us that a chair has four legs. Consequently, when we come to draw a chair, regardless of how many legs we can see, our brain will conceptualize the four-legged chair for us. It is therefore difficult to draw what we really see, because our brain will reinterpret it in the light of received wisdom.

Many of the problems generated in organizations happen precisely because current reality is not being seen for what it is, and managers instead are seeing what past experience tells them they should be seeing. So first, get your mind out of the way!

NEW PERSPECTIVES

The next stage in drawing is to look for the 'spaces' between what is being seen; in other words, to get the background right. So it is with organizational problems. If you have an issue with a particular individual look at the context or background to the problem and see if this redefines it, rather than focusing on the person first. Look at the relationships and interactions the person has with others and with the environment (in other words, draw in the light and shade).

Another way of getting a new perspective on a drawing is to turn the picture upside down and see what it suggests. In organizational terms, this process might mean putting yourself into the shoes of a customer or client and observing the treatment that the organization gives out in reality (as opposed to the assumptions those within the organization have about how they are perceived). The essential thing is to accept that our minds do not know everything and that we must be able to live with the tension and discomfort that this may produce.

Making the most of the creating process involves a fairly long initial period of playing around – literally – with possibilities. Charles Handy, in his many books on organizations, gives myriad examples of this. One example is his idea of a 'life contract'. Why should we all work 40 hours a week for 40 years? Why not make it more flexible? If we multiply, for argument's sake, 40 hours a week for 50 weeks a year for 40 years, we get 80,000 hours of work in an average lifetime. Why not allow people to use this allocation in whichever way they want, so that they can work double time for a year and then take the next year off? We can, of course, all think of reasons why not, but the vital thing in using a process like this is to remember that it is better to start with the possibilities and reject them for good reasons, than to never think of them at all because the status quo is all powerful.

Working outside accepted boundaries, which is what this technique demands, can produce confusion and insecurity as familiar structures and assumptions are stripped away. Some people will find this too uncomfortable, while others will find it too anarchic in an organizational context. But once the process starts, it can become addictive. Look at unemployment, for example. Unemployment only exists because employment has been defined in a particular way by modern society. Fifty years ago, colonial Africa had no unemployment problem. Now there is massive unemployment – but the statistics have not changed, only the economic assumptions. There is always work to be done – it is the categorization of work which has produced the definitions we currently use.

Following this line of thought, and accepting that much of the work done in an organization is there only to provide employment, not necessarily to directly further the organisation's aims, we can develop this idea further. Why not give the 'surplus' workers more freedom to create and maybe have more impact upon the life and purpose of the organization? Perhaps secretaries could send out memos in sonnet form, or managers produce silk screened prints to get their messages over to staff. The samurai warriors of Japan looked for excellence and quality in all they did. Modern organization claims to do the same – but perhaps it could be done with a little more originality?

The real point to take from all of this is that the act of creating can be important not only on an individual level, but also to free up the organization that those individuals are part of. The act of creating needs and demands attention and focus as it is vital to individual and organizational success, by giving opportunities for freshness and renewal in an age of constant change.

QUESTIONS

- How do you create?

- What helps you? What fears, assumptions and rules get in the way?

- What issues of yours would benefit from being renewed? How can you see them from a different perspective? What are the edges of the problems, their boundaries? What is the background – literally?

- Drawing on your past experience, what stops you seeing the reality of an issue as it is?

- What does your organization need to see anew? How can management development and training help?

- What spaces are there in your life, both at work and home, that allow you to create?

TRAINING AND DEVELOPMENT GUIDELINES

Training people in creating involves a delicate balance between the freedom of the individual to reach into him- or herself and develop individual potential fully and the requirements of the organization for stability, with creativity occurring within clearly defined parameters. However, this represents a perennially important issue for trainers who regard themselves as developers of people. In designing exercises and activities to release participants' creative potential some form of guidance and control needs to be built in to ensure that this balance is maintained, but often the only way that this can be done properly is by continually monitoring the processes of the activities. In other words, the trainer needs to adjust the activities as they are being practised and not lose control.

Training in creating involves allowing individuals freedom to explore their own potential for creating, while keeping the control outlined above. This can usually be achieved by ensuring that, however divorced from organizational life is the type of creative activity being indulged in, it always has a *purpose linked to the activities of the organization*. So a training menu designed with creating in mind might well draw not only on standard creativity techniques such as brainstorming but also on hands-on activities involving machinery; role plays and rehearsed dramatic scenes; painting; or physical activity. One large, well-known company used to send selected groups of delegates on silk-painting courses to help develop their managerial skills.

The trainer also needs to be aware of all the barriers that exist to the process of creating, such as the fear of being wrong, of making a fool of oneself, or of being seen as less than adequate. This can be especially true of those who have been taught throughout their lives that they are uncreative. Trainers need to help such individuals rise above these strong messages and accept the fact that everyone is capable of contributing in some unique and original way.

This is equally true of trainers. It can be difficult sometimes to risk running training programmes in ways that are original because of pressures to repeat training activities that others have used successfully. It can also be very difficult to keep your nerve when participants are reacting negatively because they are having to face their own doubts and confusions, and to keep supporting them when they are blaming you for their own anxieties. If the trainer has confidence in his or her own creative abilities and can persevere then the results for participants and trainers alike can be equally rewarding.

Specifically then, review all the training activities with which you are involved. Which follow a tried and tested path? Which would benefit from experimentation? Which areas would benefit from risk-taking? And, most importantly, how do you as a trainer feel about your own creativity and the confidence you have in yourself?

POSITIVE THINKING

This section continues the theme of using the power of our own minds to move beyond the conventions which tie us down. Specifically, we want to examine the way that we as individuals code and store the information that we receive – and the impact that this has on the way we work. There are several approaches to this topic – none of them, whatever claims may be made to the contrary, particularly new.

Neuro-linguistic programming, often known as NLP, is one such technique. Put simply, NLP looks at the way we programme our minds. *Assertiveness* as a term covers a multitude of sins, but is essentially about particular ways of looking at and interpreting the world. The third example we examine is *prosperity thinking*, which has a lot in common with the first two approaches. The message they share is that what you expect is usually what you get. If you wake up one day in a foul mood and expect the world to be equally miserable, you will soon gather enough evidence to prove your case. It is very difficult to persuade paranoid people that the world is *not* out to get them, because they are usually right: all roles and relationships contain menace and threats, albeit usually in very limited amounts. However, the paranoid individual will focus on the limited amount and exclude any positives which do not fit his or her overall standpoint.

In response to this a movement was started in the United States to further the cause of reverse paranoia. This involves, simply, searching out the positives in a situation: regardless of what people do, interpret their behaviour as helpful and assume they are 'on your side'. It is, in many ways, an exercise in creating, and is guaranteed to drive hostile people to distraction as you thank them sincerely for their contribution. But while you dream happy dreams about irritating everyone in sight, we will consider the implications of these techniques for management development.

NEURO-LINGUISTIC PROGRAMMING

One of the assumptions that NLP makes is that, at the deepest level, everything has a positive purpose. Whether or not this is true is seen as irrelevant (since you could easily find evidence either way, depending on what sort of mood you're in), but starting with the positive assumption makes life a lot more pleasant. So when something happens that may not be initially to your taste, your priority should be to try to understand what may be positive about the issue in question – a process which can often save energy and reduce the pressure and stress caused by a situation. If in a meeting, for example, you are dealing with someone who keeps trying to make a point with which you disagree, trying to shut them up will usually lead to them trying even harder, and more of your energy going into blocking until one of you snaps and one of you is defeated; whereas if the other person feels their point is being acknowledged and given positive value they well be happier to move on.

In both interpersonal and intrapersonal issues, genuine acknowledgement of another person's situation or point of view frees all parties involved to be creative and move on. The relevant NLP technique here is called 'as if' – it means thinking or acting *as if* something is the case (in these examples, acting as if the world is out to do you good). People often diminish their own experience and knowledge and won't accept that they have skills in a particular area. Saying to them: 'If you *did* know what to do, what would it be?' may sound rather facile, but tricking them into using an 'as if' technique will often produce exactly the right level of skill or expertise. People usually *do* know, but don't know they know, if you know what we mean.

The set of assumptions used in assertiveness techniques are very similar to those used in NLP. Take criticism as an example:

if you are on the receiving end of criticism, and adopt a policy of believing and acting *as if* it is always useful feedback, then you will find it easier to deal with criticism – and may even begin to search it out as part of a personal continuous improvement process. Many people object to adopting this policy, saying: 'But what if the criticism is negative, or made in anger? Why should I pander to the other person by pretending it's positive?' The answer is that if you play your role to the hilt, you will very possibly (a) shame the other person into not giving you any more negative feedback or (b) gradually encourage them, through your receptiveness, to couch their criticism in more positive terms. Nothing is 100 per cent reliable, of course – and you may need to develop the patience of a saint as an additional competency – but, again, it is a positive process, and ultimately better for your blood pressure.

The uses of positive thinking as an interpretative technique employed by NLP and assertiveness are continued in the discipline known as prosperity thinking. This is a process designed originally to help individuals resolve any emotional problems they have relating to, or caused by, money – which narrows the target audience down to about 98 per cent of the population. There are not many of us who do not have issues of one kind or another to do with money, used as it is as a symbol for so much in our society – security, love, power and so on.

Prosperity thinking does not imply that everyone can – or should – think themselves into wealth; indeed, it sees a desire for wealth as a symptom of emotional imbalance. The definition that is usually offered for this technique is *never doing anything you do not want to for money* and/or *never not doing things you want to for lack of money*. Both of these statements may seem a little idealistic to those of us with mortgages to pay, mouths to feed and golf club membership fees to find. But we must not hide from the essential truth that no one *has* to work: if we *choose* to, we could wander the empty streets at dawn searching for food from dustbins. Most of us would choose not to do this – but then most of us, according to most surveys, would choose to work rather than do nothing, even if we had enough money to live on for the rest of our lives. The proposition is really to make sure that the reasons why you would work even if you did not have to are in evidence at times when you feel you *do* have to – and examining all the possibilities for maximizing that enjoyment, rather than unquestioningly collecting a salary for work that does not make you happy.

One way to start the process off is to make a list of the things that give you greatest pleasure, and then identify those pleasures that you would want to be paid for as part of your work. From there it is a matter of using creative and positive thinking to try and make it happen, or at least to allow it to be seen as possible rather than futile. It will probably be a long-term strategy, but there's no reason why it can't happen overnight.

If you find this too daunting, you can always perform a few small reframing exercises in terms of your own job. The internal dialogue might run:

'I hate my job.'

'Then leave it.'

'I can't – I need the money.'

'What do you need the money for?'

'To support my wife/husband and family.'

'You can always leave them.'

'No I can't.'

'Why not?'

'I don't want to – my family is my main source of pleasure.'

'So if you left your job you would lose your main source of pleasure?'

'If you put it like that, yes.'

'So in one way you are working for pleasure – there is an ultimate payoff.'

Simple isn't it? (Don't answer that!) Of course, your family might give you no pleasure at all. In which case why do you choose to stay with them and choose to do a job you hate? All of us – always – have some kind of choice.

The other proposition of prosperity thinking is never not doing things you want to for lack of money. Now, there will always be things that money is essential for (buying this book, for example), but how often have you heard someone say: 'I'd love to . . . (travel the world, take up hang-gliding, etc) but I don't have the money'? What this person is really saying is 'But I don't have the energy or motivation to do it.' This is the acid test for people who spend their lives dwelling on 'if only's. If you help such a person deal with the genuine possibilities which exist you can encourage them to focus their energies on what they really want to do. If someone wants (or says they want) to travel across the Australian outback, there are many and varied ways of accomplishing this: act as a courier; hitchhike to Australia; work your passage on a ship. Suggest real ways of accomplishing the goal and the genuine seeker will thank you with tears of gratitude, the insincere will raise 'yes, but's faster than you can make the next suggestion.

IMPLICATIONS FOR THE WORK PLACE

The same thing applies in a work setting when it comes to projects, new working practices, changing jobs, or anything which requires an investment of time, energy and money. Those who are genuinely committed will invest their energies in making it happen and will find the minimum amount necessary to get things moving. Those who are not truly committed will set high minimum money targets to be attained before they start. This will probably ensure that the project in question will never happen – in which case the person involved will blame lack of money. Many people make the mistake of focusing on getting the money to do something instead of concentrating on the doing of the task in question. It is energy and commitment which ultimately make things happen.

These principles are equally valid at an organizational level. Money is often cited as an excuse for organizations not doing things that perhaps they should be. John de Lorean, in his book *On a Clear Day You Can See General Motors*, describes a meeting in which senior managers voted against installing a safety device on a car to stop it flipping over at high speed, in order to keep the price of the car down. This was not because they were immoral people, but because they were driven by an overriding need for corporate success measured in terms of profitability. So organizations also have choices to make which will be conditioned by attitudes, beliefs – and money.

Prosperity thinking sees money as part of the process of accomplishing things but very much linked in with energy, energy following commitment: what you spend (time, energy, money) flows out of you, and if spent with the right attitude (openness, willingness to 'go with the flow') will come back to you enhanced. This brings us back to the point made in the introduction to this chapter. How we choose to view money, criticism, the world, other people, is critical to our progress in this world – but it is a choice we can make, rather than passively accepting our lot or finding third parties to blame. Knowing that we have a choice gives us the burden of additional responsibility, but also freedom to grow and become what we really want to be (or not, as we choose). NLP, assertiveness and prosperity techniques are all means to that end.

Before we leave this topic, as an alternative to scrutinizing theories to do with coping styles, it is worth spending some time scrutinizing instead those individuals who can truly be said to cope with change – indeed to thrive on it. Can we learn anything from these people?

The first point to note is that individuals who thrive on change have a positive self-image. This does not mean they are egotistical, simply that they are realists who are clear about, and comfortable with, their strengths as well as their weaknesses. It is a common cultural standard – at least in the UK – that we should not be bullish about our strengths for fear of being seen as immodest. But if we are not clear about our positive attributes we will have nothing to hold on to during change – and our stress and anxiety will increase.

Second, genuinely self-confident people accept that they – and others – will make mistakes: but in the case of these individuals mistakes are seen as part of the learning process. The self-confident person matches challenge to competence ('If I can do it I will, if I can't, so what?'). This realism about human fallibility is a safety buffer which stops individuals from becoming the 'Mission Impossible' type described by Will Schutz (see Chapter 5). For Mission Impossible types any mistake is a disaster because they are perfectionists; other kinds of people who deal badly with change are hostile and paranoid types, as described in Chapter 4. The hostile person says: 'This change is making everything worse – and it's all (insert suitable name here)'s fault!'; the paranoid person says: 'This kind of thing always happens to me – and there's nothing I can do about it.'

A useful skill to acquire if you have to face up to change is 'reframing'. Reframing means accepting that every situation has both positive and negative aspects, but choosing to concentrate on the positive: choosing to learn, to develop, rather than being miserable or downhearted. So an overworked executive whose train to work is cancelled can choose either to panic about all the work sitting in his or her in-tray, or to use the extra time at the station to plan a more efficient way of using the day. The worst thing that can happen if you use this technique is that others will dismiss you as a Mary Sunshine who is perpetually optimistic – but once individuals understand that we have a choice in everything we do, stress levels can decrease considerably.

QUESTIONS

- Where and with whom could you apply the 'as if' techniques? What would happen if your organization behaved 'as if'?

- What do you want to do that you have not done because of 'lack of money'? Do you really want to do it? How can you do it? (Forget about the money.)

- What do you do that you do not want to in order to get money? How can you stop doing this? What do you really enjoy doing? How can you earn money for this?

- What does your organization do that it does not want to because of the need for profit or revenue? How can it stop doing these activities?

- What projects are not being done because of lack of money? Does the organization really want them to be done? Who has the energy and commitment to do them regardless of money available?

- How can the concept of flows of energy, of money, benefit individuals and organizations? Where, as money flows, can value be added? Where are the blockages, the holding on to money and energy?

- What are the attitudes and beliefs of people in the organization regarding money? Are budgets seen as prisons for money, or as means of enabling choices and empowerment?

- Are you clear about your strengths and abilities?

- Are you willing to accept that you learn from trial and error?

- Do you understand that you *always* have a choice?

- Do you understand how you store information in your mind? And how you process it?

- Do you understand and use reframing techniques?

- Do you understand the transition curve (see Chapter 2)?

TRAINING AND DEVELOPMENT GUIDELINES

For the trainer this area can be fraught with danger: you may find yourself accused of playing with people's minds. For this reason, and because the techniques we cover here have the greatest potential for making real differences to people's lives, most of the techniques require training to make full and safe use of them. NLP techniques, for example, should only be used by those with formal training. Even assertiveness techniques, which are less directly concerned with people's beliefs, can be very threatening to some individuals and can produce stressful and adverse reactions. Prosperity thinking is often regarded suspiciously, because it challenges so many of our accepted notions.

So what should the trainer do? First, get training in any of the areas you wish to use. Second, apply the techniques cautiously and at a pace that participants feel happy with (although this may mean having to push participants' views beyond their present boundaries). Third, be aware of reactions – if there is an explosion of anger from a particular individual they may well feel threatened by whatever technique is being discussed.

Having piled on the caveats, many people will benefit hugely from workshops on this subject. Assertiveness workshops can produce highly beneficial results for participants. Ultimately, the choice of whether to use these techniques must be a decision based on the skills and confidence of the trainer and the readiness of the participants to accept these somewhat controversial concepts. It is a case of high risk–high return in terms of training results, and for some trainers this means excitement and a feeling of achievement. For others the risks may simply be too high. As assertiveness philosophy tells us: we all have a choice.

If the trainer wants to leave the techniques aside and concentrate on the basic process of accentuating the positive, you must still be prepared for massive resistance built on the habits of a lifetime. Ask participants to list five personal strengths and five personal weaknesses, and they will usually rattle through the weaknesses but find it difficult to say really positive things about themselves. The same applies to dealing with change: many individuals will tend to look at the downside rather than the benefits.

Helping people to understand that looking for the positive can help to reduce stress and make the experience of change flow more smoothly and happily is a key first step. This does not mean ignoring the negative, or being an insufferable optimist. For the trainer the maintenance of a positive attitiude is essential if he or she is to help participants eliminate the negative, which at times can be difficult to sustain. Such techniques as reframing should be a normal part of the trainer's skills and can be learned from a variety of NLP books – one of which we refer to in 'Further Reading'.

MANAGING CHANGE AND TIME

The wise man does nothing
And yet nothing is left undone

From the *Tao Te Ching*

The *Tao Te Ching* is a short collection of verses encapsulating a spirit of acceptance of the changing nature of all things and the eternal flow (guided by the Tao – that which cannot be defined but which we in the West might think of as God) gently and lovingly guiding the universe towards positive ends. If you accept and trust in this benevolent flow then you can let go and know that all will be done.

The main principle underlying these verses is *wu-wei* – difficult to translate precisely, but essentially meaning 'Do nothing and yet do everything' – a somewhat tall order, perhaps. A story illustrating the principle is that of a rainmaker who came to a Chinese village caught in a long drought. The rainmaker stayed in his hut and did nothing – much to the consternation of the villagers who were paying him. Then, after a week, the heavens opened and the rain came pouring down. When asked what he had done, the rainmaker replied that he had done nothing but absorb the wrong and make it right: in other words by working on his internal self to feel at ease and 'right' he had affected the external environment.

So it is with change when we are caught in it. We need a certain amount of detachment so as not to become dominated by our fears and worries – or indeed our hopes. This is necessary to prevent us from forcing the change process to ends which we think are essential, but which may from a broader perspective be totally wrong. In other words, keep yourself out of the frame.

This is not to say that one can't be actively involved in a process of change – but that this particular philosophy would advocate doing one's best and leaving the rest to the 'Tao'. Often the Tao is thought of as a river flowing to the sea, and any attempt to hold on to the river of change (or time) is futile. How then can we manage the flow, the process? Simply by accepting its energy – being carried by the current rather than attempting to swim upstream.

One of the main guiding principles for change management in Taoist philosophy comes from the *I Ching*, or book of changes, which people use to get specific advice on what to do. It is not a fortune-telling device: no attempt is made to predict the future, but advice is given on how to deal with the present. Organizations such as IBM have held courses which have been based on the principles of the *I Ching*. These principles are based on the two forms of energy known as yin and yang (see Chapter 5). Yin is the 'feminine' quality, yielding, receptive and passive; yang is the 'masculine' quality, rigid, active and structured (before we all get too hung up on these classifications, let us remember that men and women all have both yin and yang energy within them). Different courses of action will be made up of varying combinations of yin and yang. Yin action is to do nothing and let events take their course; yang actions tend to be more proactive and involve specific action.

Because the future is not fixed, but dynamic and flowing, any action will affect the ultimate outcome. If you consult the *I Ching*, therefore, you will get a range of possibilities. It might say if you sit by and do nothing then *X* will happen, if however you take this course of action then *Y* will happen. It also says what the wise man would be best advised to do in a particular situation.

If the *I Ching* is looked upon as a means of focusing your own thoughts on the wider range of possibilities which any change carries within it, then it can be very valuable. At the very least the philosophy broadens our Western view, and takes us away from our habitually polarized ways of looking at situations ('I must be either in complete control of change or completely at its mercy'). As with most activities, in order to succeed we need to apply a little pressure here, give a little here, push forward in this direction, not do anything in that direction.

One way in which we experience this river-like flow is in our relationship with time. Our notions of time are fundamental to our lives, our sense of purpose, the way we relate to others, and equally fundamental to the way we handle change. Not only individuals but whole countries and cultures are governed by collective beliefs about time. And yet time management as a subject is frequently treated as if time were some sort of universal constant, external to people and unaffected by their beliefs.

A typical time management programme, for example, might have as its objective the acquisition of skills in the following areas:

- Prioritizing tasks against key objectives.

- Allocating time on the basis of these priorities.

- Efficient carrying out of these tasks.

There is nothing in this agenda about enjoyment, or even quality of work. And, as many a frustrated participant will testify, much time management training simply does not work. Many jobs cannot be carved up and prioritized in the ways suggested. Time management as it is taught on most management courses ignores the role of the individual and the subjective nature of time. If we are looking for a way into this area, there are several psychological schools of thought which have made time the centre of their systems.

Transactional analysis (TA), which we touched on briefly in Chapter 3, examines the ways in which individuals structure their lives in order to avoid boredom, chiefly through the playing of various psychological games. Eric Berne, the pioneer of this school, takes TA a stage further by proposing the notion of life 'scripts' (standard patterns of behaviour which we repeat throughout our lives) in which time plays a crucial part: one script, which Berne calls 'Until', leads an individual to feel incapable of relaxing or enjoying him- or herself *until* whatever task he or she is engaged in is completely finished and closed off. The script model is linked to the concept of 'drivers' which we looked at in Chapter 3: one of the 'drivers' identified by Berne is 'Hurry up', an exhortation within the individual's head to accomplish everything as quickly as possible – people with this driver are those who feel there are never enough hours in the day.

Modern physics, held up as a model of objectivity by those who know nothing about physics, totally accepts the subjective aspect of time and mingles it with objective aspects. One way of envisaging this relationship between the subjective and the objective is to think of time as music. Music exists as the interplay of objective noise with the subjective reactions it produces in us. Music – and time – can be linear, mono- or polychronic, circular, repetitive, or any number of combinations of these.

Even within a country or culture, time means different things to different individuals. In Taoist terms, you might say we all swim in the river in different ways, at different speeds, and either with, against or across the current. The person for whom there are never enough hours in the day can be contrasted with the footballer who turns on a sixpence to divert a fast-moving ball into the goalmouth in a split second and tells the interviewer afterwards: 'It was no problem: I had all the time in the world'. Time management, of necessity, has to be seen as a wide range of skills. Some skills will be necessary for dealing with the time demands of the external world, others for dealing with our own internal thoughts and feelings. These aspects can be plotted on a quadrant as described below.

The quadrant in Figure 6 shows two types of objectivity and subjectivity. Individuals can have a preference for their own inner world (the subjective end of the horizontal axis) but their energy may flow either outwards (externalizing) or inwards (internalizing). Similarly, individuals with a preference for the outer world (objective) can have energy flowing either outwards or inwards. This model gives us four quadrants which we can use to summarize four different time temperament styles.

In the objective-externalizer quadrant the time management style is that preached by most time management courses. Time is seen as totally objective and absolute, measured by the ticking of a universal clock somewhere. The positive aspect of this quadrant lies in the ability to control and manipulate the external world; the negative side is time viewed as an inescapable fact, leading to workaholism and a sense of the powerlessness of the individual.

The subjective-externalizer quadrant governs relationships with others. The extreme expression of this temperament lies in romantic and metaphysical literature speaking of time being an irrelevance against the indivisibility of love. On a more prosaic level, this approach to time manifests itself as, for example, hours spent talking on the phone to others and a willingness to put time and effort into relationships. Its negative expression lies in a withdrawal of energy from everything other than thinking about 'significant others'. People with this orientation may have to work at not being at the beck and call of others.

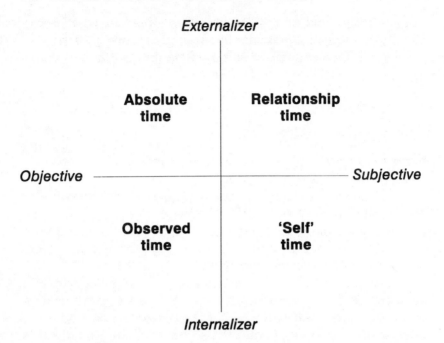

Figure 6 *Differing relationships with time*

The objective-internalizer quadrant is the home of those who see time as an objective phenomenon but see it happening somewhere else. Someone with this temperament will act as a detached onlooker, watching the flow of time from a distance and reflecting on it, or trying to understand it (in many ways this represents the objective detached position that followers of Zen try to reach). An individual with this orientation has time to look at the details of life, to complete tasks to perfection, to understand and analyse issues in depth without being dragged into the messy outer world, or having to deal with the feelings of others.

The subjective-internalizer quadrant is based upon deep values and the meaning of life, the world, relationships and ultimately spirituality. An individual who favours this quadrant will have a totally subjective perspective: his or her thoughts about time as an experience can only be expressed by the poets. People with this orientation may see time as a vehicle which takes us through a transformation: one individual with this orientation, when asked to draw a line representing his life, drew a spiral, seeing himself as moving ever closer to God.

When these different approaches are taken into account then differences in time management can be explored and played with. Some of the skills peculiar to each temperament are:

Objective-externalizer:

- Planning and organizing – controlling tasks and things.
- Doing things here and now – getting on with the job in hand.

Subjective-externalizer:

- Dealing with and relating to others.
- Making time for others when necessary.

Objective-internalizer:

- Ability to complete and finish tasks.
- Attention to detail.
- Detached and objective about time pressures.

Subjective-internalizer:

- Exploring own sense of time – enjoying experiences.
- Linking time management to own values and feelings.

To be fully effective any time management system must take into account all the different styles and skills associated with each quadrant. For example, a subjective-internalizer would tell you that concentrating on your own inner world and being clear about your innermost values may lead to external time organizing itself as far as you are concerned (like the story of the rain-maker). An objective-internalizer would advise detachment, and a subjective-externalizer would tell you to focus on the quality of your relationships rather than quantity of time in which to have them. All are equally right, and equally right as our 'traditional' time manager from the objective-externalizer quadrant.

To return to the subject of change, from a Taoist point of view it is possible that those most in danger are those who seek to regulate and control time – because any significant change will bring its own time structures and constraints with it. Any Taoist diehards in an organization which is undergoing change would advise others simply to throw away their watches and concentrate on their own inner harmony. This may not get you very far on the Ford production line, but it has as much validity as the formulaic approach to time management as it is usually taught. When involved in change, its lessons are particularly useful: stand fast and allow change to flow without being over- whelmed by it. So, trainers of the future, throw away your watches and clocks and experience what happens – now!

Of course experiencing the present, desperately rewarding though it may be, is not always enough in a world of change in which we are constantly asked to reappraise the past and plan for the future – even when we don't know what that future may be. It can be very useful to look at how we as individuals measure and store our impressions of time and how this affects our perceptions of change. In neuro-linguistic programming (NLP), which we met earlier in this chapter, a major section of work is now devoted to 'timeline therapy', the first stage of which looks at how time is stored.

You can try this for yourself by thinking of an event which happened some time ago, then a more recent event, then some- thing that is happening now, and finally something that will happen in the future. It is important to keep the events pretty much the same in terms of content – something trivial like brushing your shoes will do. Imagine doing them all together: where would the past, present and future events be located physically in relation to you? Most people, but not all, would see time as a continuum, often with the future being stored in front and to the right, and the past to the back and left. These patterns will be different for different people. They will also vary in terms of brightness, clarity and the emotions associated with different parts of the line.

Once your personal timeline is established then dealing with change can become more coherent. For example, take an antici- pated change and think about where and how it is represented on your timeline. Is it firmly fixed in the future? Does it intrude in the present? How much space does it take up compared to a change that has been successful in the past? Can you use the impressions about the change in the past to help you relate to the change you are anticipating in the future? To picture it in a less threatening way?

It can be instructive to look at the different ways we store time for different areas of our lives. Work time may be pictured as linear, or as a series of boxes, while time spent with loved ones may be seen as a sparkling continuum that flows on regardless of whether we are with them or not.

If you develop the idea of time existing as a traceable route within your head, you can use the timeline to revisit past experiences, good or bad, and review them in terms of key learnings; you may find you can bring forward skills you used in the past but had forgotten about – this is a technique often used in career counselling, which seeks to draw together what are often quite disparate chunks of experience and training into a coherent whole which takes the individual forward into new courses of action. Much selection work is also carried out with a similar aim of reviewing people's lives to see what patterns they have established for themselves, and whether these patterns relate to the future they may or may not have within the organization.

One of the most useful of the techniques which use your own representation of time is future planning. To do this you take a ride into the future (in your imagination, we hasten to add) using your timeline. If you want to bring about a specific outcome, imagine a time in the future when you have accomplished the chosen outcome and see what qualities and abilities you need to bring it about. What does the future look and feel like following the accomplishment of your objective? Does the 'you' who has succeeded have any messages for the 'you' that has yet to try? Use this information to make decisions about particular skills and abilities you may need before you attempt your goal – or even what you need to stop doing. In a very real sense you are mentally rehearsing for the future – which is a key element in successful change.

This is a very simplified account of what in NLP is a complex system of representation. In NLP, as in some of the other areas we have tackled in this book, a little knowledge can be a dangerous thing. The key point is that we are not helpless in the face of change: if we cannot change what happens to us, at least we can change how we react to and use the change for optimum benefit.

QUESTIONS

- Thinking about changes you have undergone, how did (or do) you react?

- Do you go with the flow? Resist? Push too hard? Give up?

- What do you find easy in terms of change? Hard?

- How would these Taoist principles benefit you in your everyday work – if at all?

- Do you understand how you (and others) use both 'subjective' and 'objective' time?

- What time quadrant do you most prefer using?

- What are the consequences of this?

- What time management skills do you need to improve?

* Do you understand how to use the 'Tao of Time' principles – living in balance; having a clear purpose; using continuous choice – to design your time appropriately?

- How do you store time?

- How does a past successful change contrast with an ongoing change?

- What skills and abilities did you use in the past to make change succeed? How can you use those past skills now?

- Are your views of time different for work, leisure and relationships?

- Imagine some future event that you want to happen. What do you need to start doing/stop doing/continue doing right now, in order for it to happen?

TRAINING AND DEVELOPMENT GUIDELINES

The philosophy of the Tao is one that says if you let go and trust, then all will work out well. In practical terms this means accepting that sometimes, especially if a training event is having a powerful impact, the flow of the workshop will run in ways that were not planned but which ultimately will be more beneficial. With impactful events strong negative reactions can arise; if participants are listened to and allowed to express those fears or anger or grief then the flow of the event will be much improved.

Trainers who subscribe to this philosophy accept that control of a workshop is not exclusively theirs, but flows from them to participants and back. Any attempt to hang on to control will fail. It is not necessary to accept the principles of the Tao or any Chinese philosophy to understand this group dynamic; being open to what happens in a group is enough. This 'alternative' philosophy simply brings us back to the fact that ultimately the most valuable skills a trainer can possess are sensitivity to and understanding of interpersonal interactions, and a willingness to stand back from control and be a true facilitator.

The implications of our material on time management are quite profound. It suggests that trainers need to broaden to a considerable extent their available time management material and techniques. Instead of concentrating on control through prioritization, it is important to find and develop appropriate exercises to match and nurture the many other kinds of time management skills – assertiveness, for example, to deal with that other thief of time, the interruption.

It is also important to understand the different views of time that individuals hold and resist treating time as if it were just an objective measurement. People's response to the passing of time will vary depending on mood, personality type and so on, and these need to be allowed for. Another crucial factor is the link between people's values and goals and the use they make of the time available to them. Quality rather than quantity of time is an area trainers can usefully focus on. This can lead to issues to do with relationships, work satisfaction, life goals – time management as a training event has the potential to make an enormous impact on the lives of individuals if it is 'taught' in the context of the whole person. In other words, time management – especially in the context of change – needs to be seen as an integral part of people's whole lives, not just as a set of techniques.

The use of timelines as a means of analysing the past and planning for the future is a new way of approaching time management issues, at least in the form that it is used in neuro-linguistic programming. However, it has been around for a long while in training through the use of 'lifelines'. In this technique, participants are asked to draw a line to represent their life. Sometimes they are asked to extrapolate this into the future. The discussion arising from this process is the most fruitful part of the exercise, as people examine and explain what criteria they used at the time to judge the highs and lows of their lives.

Whichever technique is used, however, the underlying themes throughout this chapter return the trainer to looking at time in many and different ways; to the importance of using as wide a variety of skills and techniques as possible to help people cope with change and time, and not sticking just to the generally accepted pathways. In other words, the trainer needs to 'go with the flow' a bit in order to find the most appropriate way to help each individual achieve his or her goals. A worthwhile objective for any trainer whatever field he or she is in!

FURTHER READING

The new science of complexity is excellently represented by two recent books. First there is Waldrop, M (1993) *Complexity*, Viking, a long book concentrating mainly on the scientists developing these new theories. Then Lewin, R (1993) *Complexity – Life at the Edge of Chaos*, Dent. This concentrates more on the theories, especially implications for life in all its manifestations in history, evolution and society.

Fritz, R (1991) *Creating*, Fawcett Columbine (New York), takes a clear line on what the author sees as the limitations of 'creativity' as it is generally taught, and is more concerned with the act of creating and the positive contribution it can make to an individual's experiences.

Ferguson, A (1992) *Creating Abundance*, Piatkus, is a highly original and thought-provoking examination of the way we regard money and wealth, and our own role in what happens to us (or rather what we collude in bringing about). Townend, A (1991) *Developing Assertiveness*, Routledge, has a number of assertiveness techniques, including reframing, which further enhance and build upon prosperity thinking. And the NLP approach to reframing is well covered in Grinder, J and Bandler, R (1979) *Frogs into Princes*.

There are several versions of the *I Ching*, or book of changes, but the classic translation is that of Baynes, C (1968) *The I Ching or Book of Changes*, Routledge & Kegan Paul. Linked with the concept of flow and the Tao is the other Chinese classic, translated by Ta-Kao, C (1959) *Tao Te Ching*, Unwin. Short and clear, the verses require much thought, like riddles designed to develop your thinking processes. Similar but more evocative are the Japanese *Haiku*, Peter Pauper Press (New York, 1965). Finally on the Tao, there is an amusing and witty exploration of the paradoxes and questions raised by the Tao and change: Smullyan, R (1977) *The Tao is Silent*, Harper & Row.

On time management there is a workshop manual by Lewis, R (1991) *Time Management Skills*, Kogan Page, which broadens the scope of time management training into a number of areas besides pure prioritizing, planning and organizing (such as dealing with others, and self-motiavtion). The most provocative book on time management for our money is Hunt, P and Hait, P

(1991) *The Tao of Time*, Simon and Schuster. It is well worth reading, if only to raise issues about the way in which time is perceived. Finally for pleasure, and to extend the analogy of time and music, Hamel, P O M (1976) *Through Music to the Self*, Element Books, is a fascinating exploration of music in different cultures and its effects on individuals and groups.

CHAPTER **7**

Afterthoughts

7 AFTERTHOUGHTS

We were on the verge of calling this final section 'Conclusions' before we realized that we were doing exactly what the spirit of this book rejects: following an accepted convention without questioning it. After all, what conclusion could there possibly be to a book which goes out of its way to open boxes without closing them, and whose introduction exhorted its readers to treat the book as a starting point rather than a be all and end all? However, this point marks the end of your journey through the ideas we have presented; like the heroes and heroines of the myths, we would love you to have gained a prize of incalculable value. But on the other hand. . .

We have to accept the realistic standpoint that this book, if used properly, will create more work than it saves. If you are stimulated and inspired by any of its ideas, it is now up to you to decide how to make those ideas work within your own context. The conclusion, therefore, is really for you to write. However, there are a couple of services we can offer on these final pages. One is to attempt to draw together some of the common themes and threads which run through the book; first, though, we would like to suggest some criteria for evaluating the potential management development initiatives which may have been suggested by what you have read.

First, while it may be personally important to you whether you agree with the thoughts of the 'gurus' – for want of a better cliché – you have met here, ours is a pragmatic view which says that even 'wrong' ideas may lead to useful outcomes. So it is worth separating your personal evaluation of the ideas themselves from any professional evaluation of their relevance and applicability. Are these models of use to you in guiding and developing your management development initiatives and strategies? If you can find no practical use for an idea, then leave it alone – however attractive it may be philosophically.

Second, do the messages and learnings from what you have read help to widen horizons, expand minds, change perspectives? Do they enable or encourage people to take a second look at their assumptions and values? We would regard this process as vital, because so many of the average individual's long-term beliefs are acquired from parents or others (like hereditary disorders or infectious diseases) without ever being questioned or challenged. If an individual questions his or her beliefs and as a result reaffirms them, then they become not only more conscious but also can be felt to be truly 'owned' by the individual in question. If left unquestioned, unconscious values and assumptions can get in the way of more consciously desired and desirable outcomes. For example, many people associate a scruffy appearance with sloth and indolence – a relationship that is totally unproven. So when Steve Jobs, the founder of Apple (in his earlier days) or some other genius comes along dressed as if for a night shovelling rubbish they may well be dismissed by the person who has not examined and challenged his or her own values. Doubtless Lord King of British Airways now regrets the time he said that he would take Virgin boss Richard Branson more seriously if he wore a suit and tie instead of his ubiquitous pullovers – a statement which clearly demonstrates a misguided priority of personal values over business acumen.

We would invite the reader, then, to judge what we have offered by these two key criteria – whether it is useful, and whether it broadens and deepens your personal perspective. So now we have the criteria, what is the sum total of what we are inviting you to judge? We would suggest looking at the content of the book in terms of five central themes:

1. Going with the flow   This central Taoist principle has cropped up many times, and is worth emphasizing because, as a phrase, it is equated by most people with a lack of productivity, with laziness: and yet some of the areas in which we see this principle at work are the epitome of precision and strength. Martial arts, for example, depend on the idea of using the energy of your opponent, working with it, not blocking it, but capturing it and turning it to your advantage (this is the physical principle behind the Judo throw); and during a recent televised soccer match the commentators spent much of the half-time conversation describing the genius of player Glen Hoddle as lying in his ability to use the flow of the ball's energy, capture it, and turn it into a devastating shot at goal without breaking his own rhythm, this technique giving him the demeanour of someone with all the time in the world.

Sportsmen, actors, creative artists of all kinds can testify to the fact that their effectiveness increases when they stop 'trying'. In other words, if you struggle consciously to get something right, you block the creative flow that leads to true efficiency; but if you allow ideas to come up by themselves and then harness them, the results are more 'natural' and of higher quality. In other words, more haste, less speed. (And how many readers have heard of cases where couples 'trying for a baby' go for years and years without success, only to conceive the moment they decide not to bother?) If you find the idea of flows of energy and spirit too esoteric, then the Alexander technique's attitude is in fact no different: when you try to do the right thing, you run the risk of overcompensating and adopting a false approach; whereas if you go with the flow but avoid doing the wrong thing your efficiency increases. This is also not very far from the basics of continuous improvement, which looks to eradicate incrementally those aspects of process or performance which hinder efficiency, while emphasizing the 'flow' of work as the heart of the process.

2. Choice and responsibility Anyone who is truly to benefit from being developed as a manager, anyone who really wants to make the best of him- or herself, has to accept that we as individuals are ultimately responsible for what we get out of life. If we choose to see good in everything, life can be good; if we choose to see bad in everything, life is one long moan – not only because of the way in which we interpret the world and choose to see it, but because of the very different kinds of signals that we send to others, who will pay back to us what we give them. If we choose to stay in a job we hate, we must either choose to make the best of it or choose to bellyache about it day after day, until our friends choose to socialize with someone else, and our family choose to relocate to Grandma's. It would be too idealistic to pretend that everyone will pay back a sunny outlook with kind words and a merry wave (there really are some bastards out there . . .) but the way in which we choose to deal with negative people will be helped or hindered by the way we choose to interpret the world.

3. Honesty   Too few organizations treasure honesty as a corporate value – with the result that everyone working in an organization finds it easier to hide the truth than face it. The most important aspect of honesty is being honest with yourself first and foremost, and then sharing that honesty with others. This is a theme we have touched on throughout the book: individuals looking at their prospective career paths have to be true to themselves if they are to find a really good fit with their employer; effective leaders, and those who thrive on change rather than sink beneath it, are generally people who are not only honest about their strengths, but prepared to acknowledge their weaknesses too; effective communication among individuals and team members relies on a degree of openness and trust; and truly productive coaching partnerships require open and honest two-way feedback.

There is a story about a large US company (which shall remain nameless) which produced electrical household goods. One day its research team came up with an idea for a waterless washing machine, which worked by using ultrasonic vibrations to shake the dirt from the clothes. The boss was hugely enthusiastic, and the research team was given an unlimited budget to develop the product. A few weeks in, the scientists realized that this machine, if it was ever to work, would have to be the size of the average living room, and would require the electricity supply of a small town. But no one had the heart to tell the boss, and so for the next two years the team went on developing, spending millions of dollars, and turning up to meetings to tell the boss how well it was going. One day a bright young science student, working with the team on a secondment, interrupted one of the meetings with the boss (just after everyone had finished enthusing) and said: 'But surely this will never work: it'll have to be the size of a living room and . . .'

4. Fear of failure   This relates directly back to honesty and why it is so difficult to achieve. How can I be honest about my shortcomings? Surely I'll lose my job? I can't possibly ask my colleagues to help me rehearse this sales presentation, even though, if I'm honest, I don't feel prepared: what if I say something stupid? They'll wonder why I was ever chosen to present.

I daren't give my opinion of this new project that's just been proposed – everyone else probably thinks it's wonderful and I'll be thrown off the team (if you haven't met it before, this is known as the Abilene Paradox – in other words, how do we know that everyone round the table nodding enthusiastically at this project isn't secretly thinking exactly the same thing?)

Basically, if you worry seriously about failing, you never start. We would bet that there is no one in the world who doesn't secretly fear failure: now if we could all be honest with each other about that, the problem would disappear overnight.

5. Wholeness This is the unifying theme which binds the others together. Carl Jung thought of perfection not as some abstract pristine state, but simply as completion. Wholeness means being honest about all aspects of human nature, not excluding anything when attempting to understand and develop individuals. It also means that nothing should ever be discounted as a possibility for adding value to the business. Beauty, for example, has the power to move people in deeper ways than money – why should it not be as great a measure of business success as profit? Many of the great scientists, Einstein among them, saw beauty and elegance as the key criteria for judging their theories – so why not business?

Wholeness is about removing the artificial boundaries that are used to separate work, leisure, social activities, love, spirituality and any of the other pigeonholes we use to put the bits of our lives into. Good business practice, and by implication management development, draws no such boundaries. Many people go to work to find love – that is a business reality. To ignore it in favour of looking solely at efficiency is to limit effectiveness and keep business and life in separate compartments. To deny, or limit your experience in, one part of your life is to impoverish the self. So maybe romantic life needs to include measures of efficiency if it, too, is to achieve wholeness.

So what are the last words? 'What works for you?' is both a good question and an appropriate statement. What does work for you? How can you build upon it? Which of the many philosophies and techniques examined in this book add to your wholeness and balance in terms of being an excellent individual, management developer and trainer? If it works for you then great, do more of it, have more and follow up the references we have given. If it doesn't, at the very least you will have reaffirmed the validity of your current approaches simply by having considered and rejected genuine alternatives, and can now go back to what really is most suitable for you. In either case we wish you well.

INDEX